# Deficit Government

# DEFICIT GOVERNMENT

*Taxing and Spending in Modern America*

## Iwan W. Morgan

*The American Ways Series*

IVAN R. DEE  *Chicago*

DEFICIT GOVERNMENT. Copyright ©1995 by Iwan W. Morgan.
All rights reserved, including the right to reproduce this book or
portions thereof in any form. For information, address: Ivan R. Dee,
Inc., 1332 North Halsted Street, Chicago 60622. Manufactured in
the United States of America and printed on acid-free paper.

Library of Congress Cataloging-in-Publication Data:
Morgan, Iwan W.
    Deficit government : taxing and spending in modern America /
Iwan W. Morgan.
        p.   cm. — (The American ways series)
    Includes bibliographical references and index.
    ISBN 1-56663-081-9 (acid-free paper). — ISBN 1-56663-082-7
    (pbk.)
    1. Budget deficits—United States.   2. Government spending
policy—United States.   3. Fiscal policy—United Stated.   I. Title.
II. Series.
HJ2051.M654   1995
339.5230973—dc20                                        94-46129

*To the memory of my father and mother
David and May Morgan*

# Contents

*Preface*    ix

1 The Budget in Historical Perspective    3
The era of balanced budgets. The age of deficits. The making of budgetary policy. Budget statistics and the historian.

2 The Making of the Modern Budget, 1933–1945    19
Roosevelt's fiscal inheritance. The New Deal and federal spending. Taxing times. The crucible of war.

3 The Age of Equilibrium, 1945–1960    55
Balancing the budget. Uncle Sam's leviathan. Consolidating the New Deal. The management of prosperity.

4 The Age of Activism, 1961–1968    86
The new economics. Defense, doctrines, and dollars. The Great Society. Guns, butter, and inflation.

5 The Age of Uncertainty, 1969–1980    115
The political economy of stagflation. Losing faith. Spend, spend, spend! Tax troubles.

6 The Age of Excess, 1981–1988    148
Reagan revolution. Dealing with the deficit. Warfare versus welfare. The Reagan deficits—malign or benign?

7 Deficit Government: The Present, the Future—and the Past    182
Taming the deficit monster. Beyond the red peril. The historical record.

*Recommended Reading*    203
*Index*    207

# Preface

THE BUDGET DEFICIT has become one of the dominant issues of American politics at the turn of the twenty-first century. The fear grows that unless the federal government puts its financial house in order, the United States will experience inevitable economic decline.

But deficit government is not a new experience for the United States. It has been a way of life since the Depression decade of the 1930s. Among modern presidents, Franklin D. Roosevelt, John F. Kennedy, Richard Nixon, Gerald Ford, Jimmy Carter, Ronald Reagan, and George Bush never succeeded in balancing the budget. Only eight times since 1933 have the final budget tallies been written in black rather than red ink. Harry S. Truman managed this feat four times, Dwight D. Eisenhower three times, and Lyndon B. Johnson once.

With the exception of the World War II era, however, budget deficits were moderate in scope until quite recently. It was in the 1980s that they mushroomed to alarming proportions. The United States today is trying to redress the legacy of this period of fiscal excess through a combination of tax increases and spending cuts.

This book examines the development of federal budgetary policy from 1933 to the present. It deals with the three main components of this policy: the money costs of government; the raising of tax revenues to pay for these; and fiscal policy, namely, the use of the budget to manage the economy. It seeks to explain how deficit government became part of the American way and to place the current fiscal problems of the United States in historical perspective. The first chapter establishes a framework for understanding the evolution of budgetary policy. The remaining chapters deal with the main periods of modern budgetary history and focus on major themes (1) the persistence of deficit budgets since the 1930s; (2) trends in federal spending and taxation that have underlain the development of deficit government; (3) the economic effects of deficits; (4) the changing terms of political debate as to whether deficit budgets are a virtue or a vice; and (5) why the 1980s marked a watershed in the history of deficit government.

In writing this book, I have—like the American government—accumulated large debts. Fortunately, these are debts of gratitude that are more pleasurable to repay than financial ones. Since this is a work of synthesis, I am heavily indebted to many scholars whose works have influenced my perspectives on the U.S. budget and are duly acknowledged in the Note on Sources. Two colleagues at London Guildhall University also provided important assistance. Peter Mandler read the whole manuscript and made valuable suggestions about how it could be improved and clarified. Bob Self's knowledge of British political economy in the 1930s and 1970s helped me better to understand American developments during these crucial periods. I am also grateful to Andrew Moran, one of the few people on this side of the Atlantic who shares my interest in U.S. budgetary history. Our many discussions on this topic helped me a great deal. Finally, thanks are due to my wife Theresa and children Humphrey and Eleanor for ensuring that family life did not run a deficit while this book was being written.

I. M.

*London*
*January 1995*

# Deficit Government

# 1

# The Budget in Historical Perspective

THE 1930s MARKED a distinctive turning point in America's budgetary history. Until this time the federal government had lived within its means more often than not. In other words, it usually spent less money on a yearly basis than it took in from tax receipts. Only one-third of the annual budgets between 1789 and 1932 were unbalanced. Deficit budgets tended to occur only when America was involved in war (which resulted in abnormally high expenditures) or when the economy was in recession (which depressed tax receipts). But the period since 1933 has been an age of deficits during which only eight budgets have been in balance.

The budget deficit has been at the center of political debate in the United States over the last sixty years. More has been at issue than the simple question of whether federal outlays and income should be balanced. The deficit problem has been entwined with matters of huge political significance relating to the role of government in modern society, how government should be paid for, and whether unbalanced budgets are good or bad for the economy. To understand how deficit government became part of the American way, it is first necessary to consider budgetary policy from a broad historical perspective. This chapter outlines America's early fiscal history, the new concerns of budgetary policy since 1933, how budgetary policy has been made, and what factors historians must take account of to make sense of fiscal statistics.

## The Era of Balanced Budgets

Balanced federal budgets became a guiding principle of American politics once the Constitution of 1787 empowered the national government to tax and spend. From then until the coming of the Civil War in 1861, they symbolized the political values of the new republic. Belief in balanced budgets was linked with belief in limited federal government, states' rights, and the nation's obligation to repay the public debt. The United States was able to live up to its fiscal ideals. A limited federal government had modest spending requirements, and its revenue needs could be met wholly from indirect taxation, mainly tariffs on imported goods.

Balanced-budget concerns remained strong in the late nineteenth century but were focused more on the problems of surpluses rather than deficits. Tariffs on imports had been substantially raised and new taxes—in the form of excise taxes, inheritance taxes, and the first-ever personal income tax—had been levied to help pay for the Civil War. Inheritance taxes and income tax were removed in the early 1870s, but excise taxes, mainly on alcohol and tobacco, were retained. In addition, the politically dominant Republican party kept tariffs at a high level to protect American industries against foreign competition. The federal government thereby took on significantly larger revenues than were needed to pay for its peacetime expenditures. The result was the longest continuous run of surplus budgets in America's history from 1866 to 1893.

These surpluses reinforced the conviction of many farmers

and small businessmen that high tariffs constituted an unfair subsidy for big business rather than a necessary source of revenue. Faced with the need to justify the tariff, the Republicans began to reduce the size of budget surpluses by spending more on public programs like internal improvements, veterans' pensions, and support for railroads. Accordingly, federal spending never returned to its very modest prewar levels (an average of $50.8 million a year in the 1850s). From the mid 1870s, when the post–Civil War military occupation of the South ended, until the mid 1890s, outlays never fell beneath $237 million (in 1878) and reached a high of $383.5 million (in 1893). In other words, budget-balancing concerns had actually resulted in the growth of national government.

Balanced-budget discipline temporarily faltered as the nineteenth century drew to an end. Between 1894 and 1915 the federal government ran fourteen deficits, compared with only twenty-nine for the entire 1789–1893 period. Two of these deficits were associated with the Spanish-American War of 1898–1900, but the others were the product of new fiscal circumstances. Federal income was no longer keeping pace with federal spending. Tax receipts were hit by a series of recessions and bank panics that affected the economy in the 1890s and early 1900s. In spite of this the federal government did not tighten its belt. Spending continued to rise and was given new impetus by the decision to finance construction of the Panama Canal, which cost $400 million between 1904 and 1916.

The reluctance to retrench was due in part to a new belief that limited government was no longer feasible. This view found expression in the Progressive reform movement, whose legacy had immense significance for budgetary policy. Its greatest contribution to American politics was to legitimize the activist presence of the federal government in the economy. The regulatory state created in the early twentieth century to oversee business practices prefigured the modern role of government in economic management. Progressivism advocated institutional reforms as the solution to the problems of urban-industrial society, rather than the big-spending social programs pioneered by a later generation of liberals. Nevertheless, its followers accepted the idea that activist government of any kind was bound to be expensive. This marked a significant departure from the traditional credo that the best kind of government was the one that cost least.

Progressivism was less concerned about how much government cost than about how it spent money. Its supporters resented expenditure programs that benefited what they thought were special interests, particularly the railroad companies, rather than the public. They also insisted that government give value for money by rooting out waste, corruption, and inefficiency in public services. As President Woodrow Wilson avowed in 1914, the American people "are not jealous of the amount their Government costs if they are sure that they get what they need and desire for the outlay, that the money is being spent for objects of which they approve, and that it is being applied with good business sense and management." Such sentiments did not entail support for deficits. The Progressives idealized a technocratic style of government run on managerial principles. In their eyes, balanced budgets were the hallmark of administrative efficiency. Accordingly, it was deemed essential to find new sources of revenue to fund the increased costs of government.

To Progressives, raising taxes on the wealthy was the only just way of increasing federal income. The first-ever corporate income tax was introduced in 1910. Three years later the Sixteenth Amendment to the Constitution empowered Congress to levy taxes on income "from whatever source derived." The Supreme Court had previously challenged such authority with regard to personal income in *Pollock v Farmers' Loan and Trust Co.* (1895). Taking advantage of this, the Underwood-Simmons Tariff Act of 1913 reduced import duties and imposed a 1 percent tax on personal incomes over $3,000 ($4,000 for married couples) and a graduated surtax on incomes from $20,000 upward. In fact, few families had an income in excess of $4,000, so at first the new tax did not produce much revenue. Customs and excise duties still generated four-fifths of federal receipts in 1915.

Substantive tax reform had to await U.S. involvement in World War I. Military exigencies provided an important impetus to the establishment of a modern tax system based on direct rather than indirect taxes and progressivity of tax rates according to wealth. Corporate and individual income taxes became the main source of federal revenue during the war. Together they produced receipts of $3.5 billion by 1919, compared with $345 million in 1916. Corporate tax hikes provided the bulk of this increase, but income tax revenues rose to $1.3 billion. The top marginal tax rate for individuals (the rate at which additions to income, such as a bonus or raise, are taxed) was sharply increased. And the lowering of the income exemption level raised the number of taxpayers from 437,000 in 1916 to 5.3 million in 1918. Other measures that enhanced the progressivity of the tax system included the reintroduction of a federal inheritance tax.

In spite of this, the new taxes did not pay for the huge costs of the war, about two-thirds of which had to be met through public borrowing. The United States operated what were then record deficits of $9 billion in 1918 and $13.4 billion in 1919. The national debt correspondingly grew from $1.2 billion in 1916 to $25.5 billion in 1919. Though this aroused great concern at the time, the relationship between war and rising debt conformed to historical trends. During the nineteenth century the United States had been involved in four wars: the War of 1812, the Mexican War of 1846–48, the Civil War, and the Spanish-American War. In each case the need to fund the military effort had greatly increased the national debt. The Civil War, for example, caused it to rise from $64 million in 1860 to $2.75 billion in 1866, an increase of 4,300 percent. But each conflict was followed by a series of balanced budgets that provided the federal government with surplus revenues to reduce the national debt. The post–World War I period was no exception to this trend. By 1930 federal indebtedness had been reduced to $16.2 billion.

Debt reduction had always been a primary motive for balancing the federal budget. This was deemed necessary to sustain the federal government's creditworthiness, to make more funds available for purposes other than interest repayment, and to fulfill a moral obligation to future generations. On this last point almost all of America's nineteenth-century leaders shared President Thomas Jefferson's view that discharge of the public debt was essential to achieve "the emancipation of our posterity from that mortal cancer." The sole dissenter was Abraham Lincoln, who regarded the public debt as a national asset provided it was largely held in American hands. "Men readily perceive," he avowed, "that they can not be much oppressed by a debt which they owe to themselves." Lincoln's outlook anticipated the modern Keynesian justification of deficits.

The desire for debt reduction remained strong in the 1920s, during which the federal government did not operate a single deficit. This was the last period of continuously balanced budgets in the twentieth century. It was also the last era of Republican political ascendancy, when the Grand Old Party controlled the presidency and Congress. The Republicans of the 1920s pursued traditional Republican tax policy. High tariff rates were restored to protect American industry and to raise revenue; corporate, personal income, and inheritance taxes were significantly reduced, though they continued to provide some two-thirds of total receipts. The so-called "trickle down" Republican economics of the 1920s held that tax concessions for business and the well-to-do would boost prosperity to the benefit of all Americans. In words that anticipated the supply-side doctrines of the 1980s, Treasury Secretary Andrew Mellon declared, "A sound system of taxation... will promote industrial and business activity by diverting into productive enterprise funds which are now going into tax-exempt securities. This should increase the number of jobs and at the same time advance general prosperity."

In contrast to their late nineteenth-century predecessors, however, the Republicans of the 1920s were determined to constrain federal spending. In part this was due to their anxiety to use budgetary surpluses to reduce the huge national debt. It also reflected their concern that government costs should not exceed a level that would require increases in corporate and personal taxes. Outlays fell from $6.4 billion in 1920 to a low of $3 billion in 1927, after which they rose slowly to reach $3.4 billion in 1930. Nevertheless, annual expenditures, excluding debt repayment, averaged over $2 billion during the 1920s, more than double the average level in the 1910–1915 period. In other words, Republican balanced budgets did not entail a return to traditional frugality.

## The Age of Deficits

Senator Hubert H. Humphrey of Minnesota, probably the foremost liberal Democrat of the mid-twentieth century, declared in 1960, "It is through the budget that we can give vital national purposes the high priority they should have in the allocation of our national resources. Through it, also, we strike a balance between public and private investment and between private and social consumption." These words could never have been spoken by any politician during the first century and a half of American history, when balanced budgets were the operative rule. Understanding why deficits became commonplace requires consideration of the new budgetary agenda that evolved from 1933 onward.

In one respect, modern budgetary policy has remained constant from the 1930s through the 1990s in its concern with the money costs of government and raising the revenues to meet these. Nevertheless, federal funds have been spent for purposes that had no real precedent in pre-1930s budgets. It is no coincidence that the age of deficits has also been the age of big government. The federal government has acquired at least three new functions in modern times— public welfare, investment in physical resources, and global responsibilities. Its success in carrying these out has depended on the expenditure of money. By contrast, the regulatory state created in the Progressive era emphasized administrative efficiency and the creation of new agencies with oversight responsibilities rather than spending powers.

A welfare state was initiated in the 1930s to provide public welfare programs within the context of a private-enterprise economy. Substantially expanded over the next forty years, public welfare became the most costly function of national government in the 1970s. Meanwhile, an investor state came into being with the rise of federal spending on transportation, resource development, energy, environmental protection, conservation, community development, and agriculture. These "physical resource" programs represented a vital investment in America's future because of their benefits for the infrastructure of the economy and the management of national resources. Finally, the anti-Communist priorities of foreign policy led to the creation of the national security state to wage the cold war in the late 1940s. Having abstained as far as possible from involvement in world affairs in the nineteenth century, the United States has been the most important actor in global politics for much of the twentieth century. The budgetary consequence of this was the massive expansion of defense spending.

In addition to providing the financial energy to drive the machinery of government, the modern budget acquired a new role that had no precedent before the 1930s. Fiscal policy became a vital instrument of economic management. Novel Keynesian doctrines legitimized the use of deficits to boost the economy during the Great Depression. The new economics of the 1960s took Keynesianism a stage further. Though the economy was not in recession, deficits were employed to maximize economic growth. The rationale for this was the full-employment budget concept, which held that federal spending should balance the hypothetical level of tax revenues that the economy would produce if it were operating at maximum capacity, rather than the actual revenue level. Keynesian policies sought to boost consumption, the demand side of the economy. In the 1980s fiscal policy developed a supply-side focus in seeking to stimulate investment. At times, however, when inflation was the main economic problem, as in the postwar era and the 1970s, the federal government ran tight budgets to reduce demand pressures within the economy.

The growth of federal activism gradually weakened the traditional ideal of balanced budgets, which became honored more in rhetoric than in practice. Many government programs proved vital to America's domestic well-being and its external security. Their money costs remained an important consideration but had to be weighed against their benefits to the nation. Every president from Franklin D. Roosevelt through George Bush aspired to balance the budget, but only three succeeded. Even those who managed this feat recognized that it could not always take precedence over other concerns of budgetary policy. As President Eisenhower acknowledged in 1953, "Balancing the budget will always remain the goal of any administration. . . . That does not mean to say that you can pick any specific date and say, 'Here, all things must give way before a balanced budget.' It is a question of where the importance of a balanced budget comes in."

## The Making of Budgetary Policy

It is a paradox that the age of deficits began soon after a new budget process was introduced to ease the task of budget balancing. In reality the federal government has operated a proper budget only since 1921. Until then Congress prepared the budget under its constitutional authority to raise taxes and appropriate funds, but it did this in a most haphazard manner. The president's role was merely to approve the legislature's revenue bills and administer the spending of funds.

Under the old system, each executive department could submit its own spending requests to the legislature at irregular times of the year. This piecemeal process made it difficult for anyone, including the president, to know the amount and purpose of every agency's funding. Budget balancing was therefore a hit-and-miss affair. The limited role of the federal government and the abundance of revenues from tariffs facilitated the achievement of a balanced budget for most of the nineteenth century. But the shortcomings of the system were exposed when spending began to outstrip revenues in the 1890s and early 1900s. The establishment of a more efficient budget process was one of the aims of Progressivism, but Congress was reluctant to cede its prerogatives. It was the need to restore budgetary stability after the huge deficit spending of World War I that finally brought about change. The fact that interest payments on the national debt now exceeded federal spending for all purposes in the prewar years rendered budget reform imperative.

The Budget and Accounting Act of 1921 established the machinery for an executive budget, thereby promoting presidential leadership in budgetary politics. It required the president to give Congress annual estimates of how much money was needed to run the government, the funding each federal program should receive, and anticipated tax revenues. This was to be done every January, and the Fiscal Year (FY) to which the estimates applied was to run from the following July 1 to June 30. (Since FY 1978 the twelve-month period has began on October 1.) The budget was named for the year in which it ended, so the FY 1960 budget, for example, applied to the twelve months that began on July 1, 1959.

The executive budget had crucial significance in setting the agenda and priorities of public policy. To the average citizen, President Johnson once commented, this might seem "a dry, unfathomable maze of figures and statistics—thicker than a Sears, Roebuck catalog and duller than a telephone

directory—which adds up to the huge outlay of his tax
dollars. In reality, it is a human document affecting the daily
lives of every American. The budget determines how many
unemployed men and women are going to be trained; how
many hungry children are going to be fed; how many poor
people are going to be housed; how many sick people are
going to be cared for; how many schoolchildren are going to
receive federal aid for books; and how our entire population
is going to be protected against a possible enemy attack."

To assist the president in preparing the budget, the 1921
reform created the Bureau of the Budget (BOB), later
renamed the Office of Management and Budget (OMB) in
1970. Originally located in the Treasury, this agency did not
realize its full potential in budget policymaking until the
government reorganization of the New Deal era. On the
recommendation of the Brownlow Committee, the BOB was
given increased resources and transferred to the newly
established Executive Office of the President in 1939.
Thereafter it played an essential role in helping the modern
presidency to control and coordinate federal spending. Staffed
by budget experts, the BOB/OMB evaluated the expenditure
proposals of each executive department and agency to ensure
that these conformed with the president's budgetary goals,
and oversaw how appropriations were eventually spent. It
also gave the president an edge in his dealings with Congress.
As government has grown, so has the executive budget
proposal, which has become increasingly difficult for anyone
but its authors to read and systematically understand. Budget
director Richard Darman admitted as much of the FY 1991
budget: "It contains almost 190,000 accounts. At the rate of
one per minute, eight hours a day, it would take over a year
to reflect upon these!"

Under the new system Congress still retained legal control

over the budget. The legislature had to approve the level of funding authorized for each program, the amount of money actually appropriated, and any change in tax law. Although this system could not deliver balanced budgets with any regularity, it did enhance budget control and ensured that deficits were small. Congress did not duplicate the president's work nor seek coequal policy leadership. In essence, it tended to accept the president's aggregates and lived within these totals while sometimes rearranging his spending priorities. Congressional budgetary discipline was reinforced by the standing committees that had jurisdiction over spending and tax bills. From the 1930s to the 1960s many of the important committees were chaired by conservative Democrats from the South, who retained strong affinity for balanced-budget traditions.

This budget process was reformed after Watergate generated a backlash against presidential power. The Budget and Impoundment Control Act of 1974 established a congressional budget to rival the president's budget. Since then the legislature has sought to set its own budgetary agenda. Reconciling this with the president's proved increasingly difficult, with the result that budgetary control declined in the late 1970s and the 1980s.

The new assertiveness of Congress coincided with the growth of party conflict over the budget. Partisan dispute in this sphere has been a feature of American politics since the 1930s, due to the budget's significance in determining the size and functions of government, which public programs had priority in terms of spending, and the level of taxes. Republicans and conservative Democrats clung to balanced-budget preferences long after deficits became the norm. From the 1930s through to the 1960s, however, political momentum lay with the mainstream of the Democratic party, which was willing to accept deficits as the price for activist government at home and abroad. It was the advent of divided party government in the late 1960s that intensified partisan controversy. Since then Republican presidents have favored tax cuts to boost the economy and domestic spending reductions to keep the deficit under control. By contrast, Democrats have used their power in Congress to protect spending programs and have increasingly called for tax increases to reduce the deficit.

The president, Congress, and the political parties are not the only actors in the making of budget policy. Also involved indirectly is the board of governors of the Federal Reserve System (known as the Fed), which has acted as the central bank of the United States since its creation in 1913. It is an independent body within the executive: the president appoints its chairman and board but cannot dictate what they do in office. The Fed has jurisdiction over monetary policy, which is concerned with managing the money supply and interest rates. This is linked with budgetary policy in several ways.

The Fed controls the money supply principally through its buying and selling of government securities, known as open-market operations. When the federal government runs a deficit, it must borrow money to fund its operations by issuing government securities, mainly Treasury notes and bonds. These can be bought by private financial institutions and by the Fed itself. When the Fed buys securities, the payments it makes for these become deposits in the Federal Reserve System's regional banks, which are then in a position to lend out more money to private banks. This leads to lower interest rates and easier credit conditions. But if the money supply grows faster than the economy, the result is higher inflation. To counter this, the Fed can contract the money supply by limiting its purchases of government securities or selling off some of those it already holds. When private banks buy securities from the Fed, the effect is to reduce the volume of reserves they have available to lend. Accordingly, the Federal Reserve's action on the money supply and interest rates have immense significance for economic policy and government borrowing. For this reason it has long been important that fiscal policy and monetary policy should not be at cross-purposes.

## Budget Statistics and the Historian

Historical analysis of the budget requires care in the use of statistics to ensure comparability over time. The first task is to find accurate data. Discrepancies in figures relating to expenditures and receipts often appear in different official publications. Probably the most accessible and most reliable source, at least for modern times, is the *Historical Tables* contained in recent editions of the budget document that the president submits each year to Congress. These provide detailed breakdowns of spending and taxation programs and present their data in a manner that ensures historical comparability for the years from FY 1934 onward.

The next task concerns the interpretation of budget statistics. One difficulty here is that ordinary individuals find it hard to comprehend the magnitude of the sums involved. The difference between a million dollars, a billion dollars, and a trillion dollars has as much relevance to most of us as the distance between the planets in our solar system. The following example may assist comprehension. If someone was handed a $100 bill every second of the day, he or she would become a millionaire eight times over within twenty-four hours. At this rate it would take 115 days to become a billionaire, and it would require 317 years to become a trillionaire.

Even if one grasps what these huge sums involve, bald statistics are of limited value to the historian. The fact that federal outlays stood at $10.8 million in FY 1800, $520.9 million in FY 1900, and $1.25 trillion in FY 1990 tells us that government spending has grown over the last two centuries, but little else. For historical comparability, two factors must be taken into consideration. First, allowance should be made for the decline in the value of money over time. Budget statistics ought to be considered in "constant" dollar terms (which are presented in FY 1982 dollars in this study) as well as current dollar terms. Thus, for example, the actual deficits of $20.5 billion in FY 1942 and $25.2 billion in FY 1968 respectively measure $152 billion and $74.2 billion in constant 1982 dollars.

Constant dollars do not provide the full measure of historical comparability. The truly important historical index for budget statistics is their relationship to Gross National Product (GNP), the total value of goods and services produced by the economy in a single year. Because the economy has grown and the population has increased over time, it is logical that the budget should keep pace. Budget growth is most significant when it occurs at a faster rate than economic growth. To illustrate this, consider the FY 1934 deficit of $3.6 billion and the FY 1980 deficit of $73.8 billion. Even though the former was far smaller in current dollar terms, it was much larger than the latter in relationship to the total output of the economy at that time. The FY 1934 deficit amounted to 5.9 percent of GNP, yet the FY 1980 deficit was only 2.8 percent of GNP.

# 2

# The Making of the Modern Budget, 1933–1945

MODERN BUDGETARY POLICY came of age during the presidency of Franklin D. Roosevelt. New Deal measures to combat the Great Depression increased the size of the budget. In FY 1930 federal outlays totaled $3.3 billion (3.6 percent of GNP). By FY 1940 they amounted to $9.5 billion (9.9 percent of GNP), the highest peacetime level to date. While the aim of New Deal spending was domestic, America's involvement in World War II transformed expenditure priorities and made defense the largest part of the modern budget. Increased spending was accompanied by regular deficits. The United States did not operate a single balanced budget between FY 1931 and 1947, the longest continuous sequence of deficits in its history until the present series began in FY 1970. Initially regarded as an embarrassment, unbalanced budgets became a positive instrument of economic policy in the late 1930s. Tax reform also featured in the making of the modern budget, and a broad-based taxation system was established during World War II. These developments may not have amounted to a fiscal revolution, but they were historically significant. By 1945 the federal budget was markedly different from the pre–1933 model.

## Roosevelt's Fiscal Inheritance

Roosevelt took office at the depth of the worst economic crisis in American history. The stock market crash of October 1929 ended the boom of the 1920s and ushered in a decade of misery. Between 1929 and 1933 unemployment rose from 3 percent of the labor force to 25 percent, while GNP fell by 30 percent, consumption by 20 percent, farm income by 70 percent, and investment by 87 percent. More than 100,000 businesses went under and over 5,750 banks failed, with a total loss of some nine million savings accounts.

Economists disagree about what caused the Great Depression, and it may be that the crisis was too complex to be explained by single causes. Keynesians argue that there was insufficient demand to sustain the productive growth of industries like automobiles and residential construction that had underwritten the prosperity of the 1920s. They blame this lack of purchasing power on the maldistribution of income, the decline of the agricultural sector, the flaws of the banking system, and the loss of wealth from the stock market crash. Monetarists, by contrast, claim that monetary mismanagement caused the Depression. In their view, Federal Reserve efforts to douse stock market inflation through interest rate increases and money supply reduction in 1928–1929 depressed the entire economy and provoked the rash of bank failures that caused the total quantity of money in circulation to fall by one-third by 1933. Other analysts blame events abroad in 1931, specifically Britain's abandonment of the gold standard, the adoption of protective trade measures by many nations (actually in retaliation against U.S. tariff increases), and a series of European bank failures. They believe these developments halted America's recovery and turned a brief recession into a slump.

Regardless of controversy over its causes, the impact of the crisis on federal finances was clear-cut. The budget moved from a surplus of $734 million in FY 1929 to a record peacetime deficit of $2.7 billion (4.6 percent of GNP) in FY 1932. The volume of federal tax receipts fell by half during this period as a result of the decline in the nation's economic activities. In FY 1932 and FY 1933 the deficit exceeded total federal revenues—unprecedented in peacetime. Meanwhile, federal outlays rose from $3.1 billion in FY 1929 to $4.7 billion in FY 1932.

The deficit budgets operated by the Republican administration of President Herbert Hoover marked the first step toward the establishment of modern fiscal policy. Hoover promoted a series of measures intended to counteract the Depression. On his recommendation, Congress reduced personal and corporate tax rates and increased public works appropriations in 1930. The president also secured legislation to underwrite credit to farmers, home buyers, and banks. His most significant action in this context was the creation in January 1932 of the Reconstruction Finance Corporation (RFC) to extend federal loans to banks and other financial institutions. The RFC was given capital stock of $500 million and total loan authority of $1.5 billion. In July of the same year it was further empowered to loan up to $1.5 billion for self-liquidating state and local public works projects and $300 billion (at 3 percent interest) to help state governments fund unemployment relief.

But these measures were utterly insufficient to compensate for the decline of the private economy. Hoover held back from large-scale spending out of fear it would spur the irreversible growth of the federal government's responsibilities. In the main his anti-Depression expenditures were indirect, involved recoverable outlays (such as loans), and did not entail permanent expansion of the budget. The RFC typified this approach. Its public works loan program financed only projects, such as bridges and housing, that would eventually pay for themselves through user fees. It would loan for relief only on the basis of "absolute need and financial exhaustion" on the part of state and local authorities. As a result of this limitation and stringent borrowing conditions, which required states to repay loans out of future federal highway grants, less than half the relief credit had been loaned by the time Roosevelt took office.

Hoover initially accepted deficits as a short-term necessity, but the extent of the Depression led him to change course. The Revenue Act of 1932, then the largest peacetime tax increase in American history, was enacted as a budget-balancing measure. Hoover's new policy was governed by monetary concerns rather than fiscal dogma. Britain's abandonment of the gold standard and devaluation of sterling, the linchpin of the world monetary system, in September 1931 had aroused fears that the U.S. would soon follow suit. As a result, foreign governments and private citizens had rushed to withdraw their gold deposits from American banks. The outflow threatened America's own gold reserve position. In an effort to allay concern about the strength of the dollar, the Federal Reserve decided to raise interest rates. But its actions were harmful to American banks, which desperately needed liquidity, and to industry, which equally needed cheap credit. In these circumstances, Hoover concluded that a balanced budget was essential to ensure that government borrowing to finance a deficit should not absorb scarce credit needed by business and thereby increase pressure for further interest rate rises.

The tax increase proved a serious mistake. Any monetary relief it brought was temporary. The Federal Reserve tightened credit conditions again to protect the dollar during the uncertain period between Hoover's defeat in the 1932 presidential election and Roosevelt's inauguration in March 1933. Moreover, the tax hike took purchasing power out of an already devastated economy, harmed small firms in particular, and further undermined big-business confidence. Nor did it balance the budget. Worsening economic conditions made nonsense of estimates that the Revenue Act would net $900 million for federal coffers in FY 1933. The gain turned out to be $100 million, which merely trimmed the deficit to $2.6 billion.

Ill-advised though they were, Hoover's efforts to balance the budget did not provoke outcry. With Keynesian doctrines still in their infancy, almost every leading economist opposed massive deficit spending. There was also partisan consensus on this score. Those Democrats and liberal Republicans who wished to expand the emergency public works program advocated tax increases or a bond issue to finance this. Nor did the Democrats question the need for budget-balancing tax increases in 1932. Instead they used their power in Congress to raise personal, corporate, and inheritance taxes paid by the wealthy and to defeat proposals for a general sales tax, which would have been borne by consumers. In terms of budgetary policy, the presidential election campaign of 1932 represented a battle for the mantle of fiscal responsibility rather than a struggle between modernity and tradition. Roosevelt berated Hoover for heading the "greatest spending Administration in peacetime" and operating a deficit that was "staggering...so great it makes us catch our breath." The Democratic candidate drew attention to his own record as governor of New York in cutting the state budget and achieving economy in government. He promised to carry on in the same vein as president. To this end,

Roosevelt avowed that he would reduce federal expenditures by one-fourth and balance the budget.

## THE NEW DEAL AND FEDERAL SPENDING

Roosevelt's inaugural address as president affirmed his belief that the federal government should adopt a more activist approach to combat the Depression without sacrificing budgetary restraint. The early New Deal did not employ fiscal policy to restore prosperity. Some of its programs, notably banking and finance reforms, antitrust measures, production codes, labor reforms, and credit liberalization, involved nonbudgetary legislative or administrative operations. But other measures did cost money, as reflected in the relatively high level of federal expenditure and continuous deficits from FY 1934 to FY 1940. Like Hoover, Roosevelt accepted deficits reluctantly as a short-term necessity, and eventually he sought to eliminate them. But the disastrous consequences of his budget-balancing efforts finally convinced him that deficits were crucial in achieving economic recovery.

FEDERAL GOVERNMENT FINANCES, FY 1934–1940 (billions of dollars)

| Fiscal Year | Budget Receipts | Budget Outlays | Deficit | Receipts as % GNP | Outlays as % GNP | Deficit as % GNP |
|---|---|---|---|---|---|---|
| 1934 | 3.0 | 6.6 | -3.6 | 4.9 | 10.8 | -5.9 |
| 1935 | 3.6 | 6.4 | -2.8 | 5.2 | 9.3 | -4.1 |
| 1936 | 3.9 | 8.2 | -4.3 | 5.0 | 10.6 | -5.5 |
| 1937 | 5.9 | 7.6 | -2.2 | 6.2 | 8.7 | -2.5 |
| 1938 | 6.7 | 6.8 | -0.1 | 7.6 | 7.7 | -0.1 |
| 1939 | 6.3 | 9.1 | -2.8 | 7.1 | 10.3 | -3.2 |
| 1940 | 6.6 | 9.5 | -2.9 | 6.8 | 9.9 | -3.0 |

Source: *Historical Tables, Budget of the United States Government, FY 1992*, p. 13, 15.

As the table opposite indicates, all of Roosevelt's budgets outspent Hoover's largest budget ($4.7 billion in FY 1932). By FY 1940 total budget expenditures were triple in real terms (allowing for deflation) what they had been in FY 1929 and about double the FY 1932 level. Only two of Roosevelt's deficits were smaller in dollar terms than Hoover's largest deficit ($2.7 billion in FY 1932). On this point it must be borne in mind that the FY 1937–1940 deficits were relatively small because the collection of the new social insurance taxes netted some $5 billion for federal coffers during this period.

Yet Roosevelt and Hoover differed more by degree than doctrine. The largest deficit incurred under FDR was only some three-fifths bigger than the FY 1932 deficit. Moreover, the dollar size of the deficit was an inadequate measure of fiscal policy because of the automatic effects of unemployment on tax revenues. In the 1950s economists developed the concept of the "full-employment budget" to assess the intentional effects of fiscal policy. This analytic tool calculates the hypothetical deficit (or surplus) that would be obtained if the economy were operating at full employment and producing the largest possible national income. It allows for proper comparison of the expansionary nature of the federal budget at different times by factoring out economic circumstances from the fiscal equation. If the full-employment deficit is higher in one budget than another, this is due to deliberate policy actions such as spending increases or tax cuts. The application of this concept to the budgets of the Depression era show that fiscal policy was less expansionary in FY 1937–1940 than under Hoover in FY 1931–1932. Only in FY 1934 and 1936 were the full-employment deficits of the New Deal budgets substantively higher than those of Hoover's budgets, and these were insufficient to boost recovery.

Taken as a whole, Roosevelt's fiscal record in FY 1934–1940 was no more expansionary than Hoover's in FY 1930–1932. Federal spending rose significantly during the New Deal era, but the stimulative effects of this were counterbalanced by the increased volume of tax receipts as the economy began to improve slowly from the nadir of 1932–1933. Moreover, total public spending in the New Deal era was barely higher than in the late 1920s because federal increases were offset by state and local government retrenchment.

The limitations of fiscal policy under Roosevelt were not attributable to the kind of monetary concerns that had influenced Hoover's actions in 1931–1932. New Deal reforms liberated the budget from these shackles by promoting an expansionary monetary policy. America's abandonment of the gold standard in March 1933 meant that interest rates no longer had to be kept high to defend the value of the dollar. To safeguard U.S. gold reserves, the export of gold was suspended in 1933 and allowed to resume only after the Gold Reserve Act of 1934 fixed the price of gold at $35 an ounce, effectively devaluing the dollar by about two-fifths. Moreover, all banks were temporarily closed in March 1933, and only those whose solvency the federal government endorsed were allowed to reopen. Other banking reforms authorized the Federal Reserve to lend to member banks without limitations on the character of the security accepted and established a program for federal insurance of bank deposits. Meanwhile, the Thomas Amendment to the Agricultural Adjustment Act of 1933 gave the president extraordinary powers to inflate the economy, including authority to require Treasury issue of up to $3 billion in unsecured paper currency and Federal Reserve purchase of up to $3 billion in government securities in order to increase credit through open-market operations. These measures put an end to worries about a gold drain, restored confidence in the banking system, and ensured that government borrowing to finance deficit budgets would not cause interest rates to rise to unacceptable levels.

Roosevelt could therefore have operated much higher deficits than Hoover without fear of crowding out business from tight credit markets. He did not do so because of his strong belief, based on economic and political reasoning, in sound finance. Since business investment had declined much more sharply than consumption, the new president and his principal advisers saw the restoration of business confidence as the precondition for economic recovery. For this reason the central thrust of the early New Deal was the attempt to provide investors with psychological and institutional supports for private-sector expansion. Deficit spending did not suit this strategy. Even in the depths of the Depression most corporate leaders equated unbalanced budgets with the threat of inflation. Their reasoning ran as follows: the rise in government borrowing requirements would eventually impair government creditworthiness; the federal authorities would then be compelled to print more money to finance government debts; and the result would be a ruinous monetary inflation. The contrary theory—that the economy had to be "reflated" before a balanced budget was possible—lacked influential adherents until the latter half of the 1930s.

The president also doubted the efficacy of spending solutions. He had stated during the 1932 election campaign: "People suggest that a huge expenditure of public funds will completely solve the unemployment problem.... Let us admit frankly that this would only be a stopgap. A real economic cure must go to the killing of the bacteria in the system rather than the external symptoms." Having entered politics in the second decade of the twentieth century, Roosevelt had been strongly influenced by Progressivism, and he continued to believe in many of its ideals. It was not surprising, therefore, that the priority of the early New Deal was the creation of new regulatory bodies like the Securities and Exchange Commission (SEC) and planning agencies like the National Recovery Administration (NRA) and the Agricultural Adjustment Administration (AAA), which addressed structural weaknesses of the American economy. Institutional reforms that sought to eliminate stock market abuses, strengthen the banking system, and create a more orderly market economy were regarded as the key to recovery.

Though pragmatic on many other issues, Roosevelt regarded sound finance as the hallmark of responsible government. His forthright election promise to eliminate deficits reflected this, and he recognized the political danger of not fulfilling it. Democrats in Congress remained overwhelmingly committed to balanced-budget ideals. Most voters held similar views throughout the Depression era. Gallup polls (which began in 1935) consistently recorded that between 60 and 70 percent of respondents were in favor of balancing the budget and reducing the national debt, even at the cost of reductions in spending.

Roosevelt nevertheless had a flexible concept of sound finance. Recognizing that the budget could not be balanced in the short term, he did not repeat Hoover's error of raising taxes to offset revenue losses. Instead, FDR required only that balanced budgets be restored as soon as the economy regained its normal vigor. To this end he distinguished between outlays on "general" programs that predated the Depression (such as defense, transportation, and debt retirement) and "emergency" spending on measures to boost recovery (such as public works and relief). Roosevelt sought to ensure that general expenditure did not exceed tax revenue, thereby demonstrating that current deficits were entirely due to economic circumstances and would disappear with the return of prosperity. He also envisaged that federal spending and the deficit should decline as the economy improved, in other words before full recovery.

This outlook enabled Roosevelt to promote a much bigger spending program than Hoover's. His belief in structural reform did not preclude recognition that the federal government had an obligation to provide immediate relief to the unemployed. This was clearly stated in the same 1932 campaign speeches promising the restoration of balanced budgets. At Pittsburgh, Roosevelt had proclaimed: "If starvation and dire need on the part of any of our citizens make necessary the appropriation of additional funds which would keep the budget out of balance, I shall not hesitate to tell the American people the full truth and ask them to authorize the expenditure of that additional amount."

Not everyone in the Roosevelt administration approved of emergency deficit spending. The president received support from Secretary of Labor Frances Perkins, Secretary of the Interior Harold Ickes, Secretary of Agriculture Henry Wallace, relief director Harry Hopkins, and NRA chief Hugh Johnson. Others, including Treasury officials and probusiness New Dealers like Raymond Moley and Donald Richberg, placed greater emphasis on balancing the budget to restore business confidence. The foremost spokesman of this group was Bureau of the Budget director Lewis Douglas, who repeatedly warned the president that the inflationary consequences of deficits could open the way for the establishment of fascism or communism in America. Douglas resigned in 1934 in disillusion with budget policy. Treasury Secretary Henry Morgenthau took his place as the champion of balanced budgets, but he was willing to tolerate short-term deficits to pay for emergency relief.

Support for spending was not based on a "pump-priming" theory that a temporary expansion of federal expenditure would promote economic recovery, nor on what Keynesians would later term the "multiplier" idea that public spending boosted private spending. Instead Roosevelt and his allies regarded spending primarily as an emergency measure that met immediate relief needs while the foundations of renewed prosperity were being laid by New Deal reforms. The question that exercised the president was how much spending was needed for relief, rather than how much was needed for recovery. The FY 1934–1937 deficits did help to stimulate economic growth, but only in an inadvertent, inconsistent, and inadequate fashion.

The expansionary effect of some spending measures was blunted by deflationary accompaniments. In May 1933 Roosevelt obtained a $500 million appropriation for emergency unemployment relief. This was precisely the saving yielded by the recently approved Economy Act of 1933, which cut federal salaries and payments to veterans. Similarly, the Agricultural Adjustment Act of 1933, designed to raise farm commodity prices, introduced federal payments for farmers who reduced acreage in basic crops—but this was financed by a special tax on food processors, who passed on the cost to consumers.

The New Deal's most important contribution to the modern welfare state—the Social Security Act of 1935—was also one of its most deflationary measures. The act created two social insurance programs. Old-age insurance (to be first paid in 1940) was financed through a payroll tax that both employees and employers paid in equal amounts into a special federal trust fund. Unemployment insurance was financed by a state tax on employers, whose proceeds were deposited in each state's account in another federal trust fund. The Social Security Act also encouraged states to establish categorical public assistance programs for the blind, the indigent elderly, and dependent children by providing federal matching funds. Washington gave each state one dollar for every two dollars it spent on the elderly and blind, and one dollar for every three dollars in the case of dependent children. But the social insurance taxes, particularly the old-age insurance contributions, took far more purchasing power out of the depressed economy than payouts mandated by the 1935 legislation put back in. Roosevelt was not blind to this problem, but he insisted on contributory benefits to guarantee the solvency of the pension scheme and safeguard its long-term existence. "With those taxes in there," he commented privately, "no damn politician can ever scrap my social security program."

The limitations of New Deal fiscal policy were further evidenced by the bonus issue. In 1935 Congress responded to the hardship pleas of veterans by approving immediate payment of World War I servicemen's bonuses that were not due until 1945. Here was an opportunity for the administration to support an income-transfer program that would put money in people's pockets far more rapidly and efficiently than existing relief programs could. Yet Roosevelt broke precedent to go personally before Congress to veto the bill on grounds that its enlargement of the deficit would be inflationary. With an eye on upcoming elections, Congress passed another bonus bill in 1936 and on this occasion overrode the president's veto. It was due in no small part to this measure, which provided a $2.2 billion payout, that the FY 1936 budget operated the largest and the most expansionary deficit of the New Deal era.

Budgetary constraints also affected every New Deal relief program, none of which spent enough to meet the needs of the unemployed. Roosevelt's anxiety about the deficit deterred him from supporting more ambitious schemes advocated by some New Dealers, notably Harry Hopkins. For this reason the tensions within the administration between the budget balancers and the spenders suited him well. The president used the former to keep the latter in check. As he admitted, "[Budget Director] Douglas' job is to prevent the government from spending, just as hard as he possibly can. That is his job. Somewhere between his effort to spend nothing...and the point of view of people who want to spend ten billions additional on public works, we will get somewhere, and we are trying to work out a program." This middle-way approach continued long after Douglas left office.

The Federal Emergency Relief Administration (FERA), created in mid-1933, was the first step toward the establishment of a federal welfare state. In contrast to Hoover's insistence on loans, it gave the states grants to fund direct relief and work relief for the unemployed: half the money was available on a matching-grant basis whereby one federal dollar was put up for three state dollars, and half was available as a straightforward grant on the basis of need. During its two-and-a-half year existence, the FERA distributed federal funds totaling $2.9 billion while the states spent an additional $1.2 billion on relief. This represented a significant advancement over 1932 when relief spending by federal, state, and local government had totaled only $208 million. Nevertheless, FERA monthly payments averaged only $25 to $29 per family in 1935, far below the $100 widely regarded as the minimum family subsistence level. Also, FERA aid never reached more than half the jobless at any time. Far more generous was the Civil Works Administration (CWA), a purely federal operation created to provide work relief during the winter of 1933–1934. It employed four million people at its peak and spent $860 million of federal money in just over four months. But Roosevelt feared that the CWA cost too much and was creating permanent dependency on the federal purse. It was phased out as soon as the economy showed signs of improvement in the spring of 1934, when all federal relief was again placed under the FERA.

Roosevelt's determination to eliminate federal involvement in direct relief led to further reorganization in 1935: the federal government would limit itself to work relief, which gave some return on financial outlays, and leave the care of unemployables in state and local hands. The Emergency Relief Appropriation Act of 1935 approved funding of $4.8 billion for federal work projects. This was the largest single appropriation to date in the peacetime history of the United States or of any nation. Senator Robert La Follette, the Wisconsin Progressive, warned that it would take $9.8 billion to put all the unemployed back to work. This prediction showed a sound grasp of economic reality but was utterly impractical from a political perspective. Neither Roosevelt nor his advisers, let alone most members of Congress, could support spending of such magnitude.

The Works Progress Administration (WPA), a new agency directed by Harry Hopkins, received $1.4 billion from the 1935 appropriation. Remaining funds went in smaller portions to diverse agencies, such as the Public Works Administration and the Bureau of Roads, mainly engaged in public construction projects that were carefully planned, used expensive materials, and were of long-term utility. By contrast, Hopkins ensured that the WPA provided maximum employment and spending in the minimum of time. With further appropri-

ations, it expended some $10 billion of federal funds by the
end of 1941. Over three-quarters of its budget went toward
labor costs, and most of its projects were small-scale ventures
that mainly employed unskilled and semiskilled workers.
Like the FERA, the WPA was never given enough money;
most of the time it was only able to help around 30 percent
of the unemployed, and its $55 monthly wage was a pittance.
Nevertheless, more than any other New Deal agency, the
WPA showed the potential of federal spending to boost
consumption and promote economic recovery.

While Roosevelt worried about the costs of emergency
relief, other recovery programs were contributing to the
permanent enlargement of spending on physical resources.
In this sense the New Deal boosted the development of the
investor state. Significantly, the FY 1937 budget transferred
expenditures on the AAA, the Civilian Conservation Corps
(CCC), the Rural Electrification Administration (REA), and
part of the public works program from the "recovery and
relief" category to the "regular" ledger in recognition of
their long-term significance. Three program areas experienced
particularly strong expansion under the New Deal. Between
FY 1932 and FY 1940 spending on natural resource development rose from $161 million to $1.8 billion, on transportation
from $414 million to $1.2 billion, and on farm income
stabilization from zero to $694 million. Their combined
share of the budget grew from 14 percent to 38 percent
during this time.

The Tennessee Valley Authority (TVA), which sought the
economic regeneration of a long-depressed region, was the
most famous example of New Deal natural resource development. As important in the long term were the 1936 legislation
establishing federal responsibility for nationwide flood control
in river basins and the Reclamation Project Act of 1939,

which mandated federal assistance in financing multipurpose water projects. The New Deal also promoted a more diversified transportation system through grants-in-aid for highway construction, subsidies for the merchant marine, and financial aid for aviation. Meanwhile, it established the framework of federal farm policy that endures to the present day. A series of measures tied the agricultural sector to the federal government for supply and price management and credit provision.

At the start of Roosevelt's second term full economic recovery seemed to be within sight. Though unemployment remained around 14 percent, GNP was only some 10 percent beneath the 1929 level. The pump-priming effects of New Deal spending had fueled economic growth. Other factors had also helped. American exports benefited from the recovery momentum in other nations and from the rise in world commodity prices. More important, Roosevelt's gold policy, which had pegged the dollar price of gold at a high level, brought $4 billion in new deposits from Europe in 1934–1936. The increase in gold reserves produced an extremely rapid expansion in the money stock, which boosted credit and consumption. But this promising situation came to an abrupt end in mid-1937 when the United States experienced one of the most severe economic downturns in its history. During this recession, which lasted until mid-1938, industrial production fell by a third and national income declined 13 percent. The primary cause was the mismanagement of monetary and fiscal policy.

Fearful that recovery would generate inflation, Federal Reserve authorities increased reserve requirements for member banks in late 1936. The Treasury also adopted a "sterilization" policy to prevent the growing stock of gold from expanding bank reserves. The aim was merely to shrink excess reserves, but the effect was to reduce bank credit and the money supply, with the result that interest rates rose. To maintain their reserve positions, banks curtailed lending, which undermined business confidence, and began selling their investments, one effect of which was to drive down the price of government bonds. To make matters worse, fiscal policy was also changing course. The collection of Social Security taxes beginning in 1937 reduced workers' purchasing power. The recent imposition of new corporate taxes, especially on undistributed profits, had a deleterious effect on business confidence. Meanwhile, the administration planned a balanced budget for FY 1938 in the belief that continued recovery would boost tax receipts and permit reduced spending on relief. Expenditure was also scheduled to fall because the veterans' bonus had been paid off. The monetary situation only made Roosevelt more anxious to balance the budget in order to defend government creditworthiness in the volatile securities market. Even Federal Reserve chairman Marriner Eccles, hitherto an advocate of deficit spending, now urged this course of action. But the combined effect of monetary and fiscal restraint produced a recession within the depression.

The president was faced with a stark choice between adhering to his balanced-budget preferences and spending his way out of "the Roosevelt recession." Treasury Secretary Morgenthau, backed by conservative cabinet members like Postmaster General James Farley, urged him to hold fast. The recession, they argued, showed that business did not have the confidence to invest, but a balanced budget would do much to secure this. For Morgenthau, in particular, a balanced budget was now necessary to preserve the New Deal's political legitimacy. In his eyes it had now become the essential means to generate recovery rather than a signpost that recovery had occurred. By contrast, Hopkins, Harold

Ickes, Henry Wallace, Eccles (who had returned to the ranks of spenders), and a host of younger New Dealers spread throughout the federal bureaucracy, notably Lauchlin Currie, Mordecai Ezekiel, Leon Henderson, and Aubrey Williams, advocated a fiscal policy that was basically Keynesian.

British economist John Maynard Keynes did not publish his great work, *The General Theory of Employment, Interest and Money*, until 1936, but his ideas were already known in America as a result of his energetic efforts to popularize them. Some aspects of his thinking had also been foreshadowed a decade or more earlier in the works of J. A. Hobson, Stuart Chase, and William Truffant Foster and Waddill Catchings. In essence, Keynesian doctrine and its antecedents held that consumption was more important than production as a generator of modern economic growth; that recession resulted from underconsumption; and that public spending was the best vehicle to achieve recovery. This utterly contradicted the orthodox theory that production created its own purchasing power.

To Keynes, government expenditure in a recession had to be compensatory, in other words it should make up for the decline in private economic activity, and this inevitably necessitated deficit budgets. Where Keynes broke entirely new ground was in advancing the multiplier theory to justify this. It argued as follows: if the government borrowed money and paid it in some form or other to previously unemployed workers, they would quickly spend it on the necessities of life; those to whom workers paid the money would then respend their portions, at a rate estimated by Keynes to yield at least a doubling of the original outlay by government. In other words, deficit spending would have a chain reaction that would revitalize the economy. The boost it gave to consumption would lead in turn to reduced unemployment, increased production, the restoration of business confidence, and the revival of capital investment in industry. Keynes recognized that increased investment was essential for improved productivity, on which economic growth was ultimately dependent. In his view, it was the expectations of profits that generated new investment, and the key to business profitability was a high consumption–full employment economy, which could be achieved with the aid of fiscal policy.

In earlier works, such as *The Means to Prosperity* (1933), Keynes had envisaged that temporary deficits would be adequate to generate recovery and restore full employment. By 1936, however, the prolonged Depression had induced a more pessimistic outlook that underinvestment and oversaving were inherent tendencies of advanced capitalist economies. Accordingly, he now warned that there might be a permanent need for unbalanced budgets to sustain prosperity.

The Keynesian rationale strongly influenced liberal New Dealers, whose confidence about economic recovery had been shattered by the recession. They now feared that the nation faced an era of recurrent depressions interrupted only by weak recoveries that died in infancy—unless there was an increase in both the regulatory and fiscal activism of the state to deal with the problems of a "mature economy." The "mature economy" concept predated Keynes but gained new authority from his ideas. It rested on several arguments: the supply of new land and natural resources, seemingly endless in the nineteenth century, had run out; population growth was leveling off; and, most important, the end of "capital accumulation" was nigh, because the basic industries (like railroads, steel, and automobiles) were now built and new industrial sectors showed no signs of emerging. If the great age of industrial growth was over, the challenge facing

America was to adapt to the new age of limits. To do so, New Deal liberals argued, it was necessary for the state to ensure a more equitable distribution of wealth and resources through its regulatory powers and to compensate for the inadequacy of the private economy through greater public spending and investment, in other words by permanently operating deficit budgets.

Roosevelt dithered over what to do about the recession throughout the winter of 1937–1938, but the economic arguments of his advisers and his own worries about the forthcoming midterm elections finally persuaded him to resort to deficit spending in April 1938. A few weeks later the president sent a message to Congress calling for the appropriation of $3 billion for emergency spending and credit programs. In a fireside chat to explain this program to the American people, Roosevelt laid emphasis on the problem of underconsumption and avowed that "government had to make definite additions to the nation's purchasing power." In other public statements he spoke frankly about the virtues of deficits as the cornerstone of "compensatory fiscal policy."

The change of budgetary course in 1938–1939 marked the takeoff of the fiscal revolution, but it would not be completed until the mid-1960s. Fiscal policy finally became the primary instrument of Roosevelt's economic policy in FY 1939–1940. Nevertheless, federal outlays rose only by some $2.3 billion (2.6 percent of GNP) in FY 1939 over the deflationary budget of FY 1938. This helped to get the economy moving again but was hardly enough to restore it to full vigor. Some ten million people remained jobless in 1940. Roosevelt may have employed what were in effect Keynesian measures, but he had not converted to the Keynesian faith. Unable to make a complete break from the old-time religion of sound finance, he never reconciled himself to deficit spending as the fundamental, long-term approach to full economic recovery. As a result he pursued a half-baked fiscal policy that was doomed to fail. In the words of historian James MacGregor Burns, "The trouble with deficit spending was that halfway application did not work. It had utility only through full and determined use; otherwise it only served to antagonize and worry business by increasing the public debt without sufficiently raising spending and investment. A Keynesian solution, in short, involved an almost absolute commitment, and Roosevelt was not one to commit himself absolutely to any political or economic method."

Even had Roosevelt shown more enthusiasm for Keynesianism, it is doubtful whether he could have implemented a full-scale spending program in the late 1930s. The recession proved a political disaster for the New Deal because of the impetus it gave to the development of an informal conservative coalition in Congress. Conservative critics from both Republican and Democratic ranks, who hitherto had been forced to admit that economic conditions were getting better, were given cause to voice fears that Roosevelt's programs had damaged the well-being of American free enterprise. The Conservative Manifesto, issued in December 1937, expressed their conviction that tax cuts, spending reductions, and a balanced budget were among the preconditions for the revival of business confidence and economic growth. The failure of Roosevelt's efforts to purge conservative Democrats, together with Republican gains in the 1938 midterm elections, further weakened the New Deal. Thereafter the conservative bloc had sufficient strength to inflict several budgetary defeats on the administration.

From 1933 to 1938 Congress largely went along with Roosevelt's appropriation requests. Its solitary rebellion, over the veterans' bonus, had the effect of increasing outlays. The main disputes over deficit budgets had taken place within the administration itself. But after the emergence of the bipartisan conservative bloc, the legislature grew more active in restraining presidential spending. In 1939 it cut the relief appropriation and rejected a new antirecession loan program, even though this was intended to fund self-liquidating public works. More was at issue than differing views about economic recovery. Conservatives inside and outside Congress worried that New Deal budgets could eventually destroy the American system of capitalism. To some, the great danger of deficit finance was ruinous inflation that would sow the seeds of fascism, as had happened in Germany and Italy. Others were more concerned that its promotion of big government would eventually result in socialism or communism. Among those not discriminating between either outcome was former President Herbert Hoover, who warned that deficit spending constituted "the first step towards fascism, communism, socialism, stateism, planned economy, or whatever name collectivism happens to be using at the moment."

Such convictions indicated the importance of unbalanced budgets in American politics from the late 1930s onward. As historian James Savage observed, deficit spending now "symbolized the federal government's presence in the economy and society, a presence that was perceived to be either a bureaucratic intrusion threatening the nation's liberty or the necessary product of a responsible government's policies that provided for the country's well-being."

### Taxing Times

New Deal budget policy impinged on taxation as well as spending. The main priority of Roosevelt's tax policy was to raise money to fund his new programs. Tax receipts rose steadily from $3 billion (4.9 percent of GNP) in FY 1934 to $6.8 billion (7.6 percent of GNP) in FY 1938, but then declined as a result of the recession. Federal income amounted to only $6.5 billion (6.8 percent of GNP) in FY 1940. The revenue situation was somewhat distorted in FY 1937–1940 by the new payroll taxes, which could not be used to finance spending programs other than social insurance. Nevertheless, the social insurance trust funds operated large surpluses, which the Treasury invested in U.S. bonds. In effect, the government loaned itself money, which it promised to repay to itself in the future. This practice eased its borrowing needs and financed part of the deficit.

The revenue expansion of FY 1934–1938 was in large part a direct consequence of economic improvement, but New Deal tax policy was a hindrance rather than a help to the process of recovery. No effort was made to stimulate consumption through tax cuts. Instead New Deal taxes sucked purchasing power out of the economy and bore disproportionately on lower-income groups. A limited attempt to transfer the tax burden toward those most able to pay proved ineffective and largely symbolic.

The New Deal inherited a skewed taxation system that was the offspring of the Depression and the 1932 Revenue Act. In FY 1926–1930 tariff and excise duties, which were indirect taxes on consumers, yielded a third of federal revenues, while personal income, corporate, and inheritance taxes produced two-thirds. In FY 1934, their respective contributions were 57 percent and 31 percent. The increase in the excise duty share from 16 percent in FY 1926–1930 to 46 percent in FY 1934 was largely responsible for this transformation. The decline of incomes in the depressed economy had erased the revenue benefits of personal and corporate tax hikes mandated by the 1932 Revenue Act, whereas its selective excise levies (on motor vehicles, gasoline, radios, phonographs, and long-distance telephone calls) produced about 15 percent of FY 1934 receipts. Meanwhile, tobacco duties, largely derived from World War I, continued to generate substantial revenues (12 percent of total receipts in FY 1934–1940, about the same as in FY 1926–1930).

The Roosevelt administration maintained and expanded the system of indirect taxes. It repeatedly secured legislative extensions of the excise duties that Hoover had introduced as temporary budget-balancing measures. To these were added new duties on alcohol following the repeal of Prohibition in 1933 and a processing tax to finance AAA payments to farmers. There was only one deviation from this trend. An avowed internationalist, Roosevelt was critical of protective tariffs, and he initiated moves toward freer trade by promoting reciprocal trade legislation in 1934. Accordingly, the tariff grew less significant as a revenue source, declining from 16 percent of total receipts in FY 1932 to 5 percent in FY 1940.

The inequity of New Deal taxation did not provoke public outcry. Indirect taxes carried relatively low political risk because they were hidden. In a 1939 poll, one in four respondents, mostly from low-income brackets, professed belief that they did not pay any federal taxes. Those consumers who were aware of being levied did not consider the burden excessive because in most cases only pennies were being added to the cost of individual items. Alcohol taxes, which yielded about 12 percent of total federal receipts in FY 1934–1940, were not even perceived as increasing the price of liquor. Legal whiskey was cheaper than the bootleg variety, so the new duties did not arouse resentment among consumers. Nor was the processing tax, which accounted for one-eighth of federal income at its peak, seen as a tax on food. Though the costs were passed on to the public, the levy was imposed on none-too-popular middlemen, the food companies, rather than on producers and consumers.

The shortcomings of Roosevelt's tax policy were highlighted by the principal New Deal contribution to the modern tax system, Social Security payroll taxes. In no other nation's welfare system did government abstain from all financial responsibility for old-age insurance. Roosevelt's anxiety to safeguard the insurance program against future dismantlement by conservatives led him to insist on a funding method that would ensure both the individual's "earned right" to a benefit and the solvency of the program. Social Security has indeed survived, even proving resistant to the Reagan Revolution of the 1980s, but the means of financing it contradicted the principle of progressive taxation. Though the payroll tax operated at a flat rate, the lid on wages subject to tax and the exemption of nonwage income means that the effective rates for upper-income recipients have been lower than for other income groups. Employers are also subject to social insurance taxes, of course, a fact which enabled Roosevelt to claim that program costs did not fall exclusively on "the people." But most tax experts agree that workers have effectively borne much of the costs of employer contributions, since these are passed on to consumers in the prices of goods.

Roosevelt's initial belief that recovery would spring from a revival of business confidence predisposed him against increasing the corporate tax burden. By mid 1935, however, he had fallen out with business over the NRA and other reforms. Now there was a growing belief within the administration and Congress that the concentration of wealth in the hands of big business was hurting economic recovery because it restricted individual enterprise and opportunity. Meanwhile, populist demagogues like Senator Huey P. Long of Louisiana orchestrated grass-roots resentment of the super-rich to demand massive redistribution of wealth. The Treasury was also growing increasingly desperate for more revenue to hold the budget deficit under control. In these circumstances the New Deal made an effort to shift the tax burden to the rich.

In 1935 Roosevelt promoted enactment of a revenue law that increased the top rates of the individual income tax, sharply graduated corporation taxes, and raised inheritance taxes. The next year congressional approval of the veterans' bonus and the Supreme Court's invalidation of the AAA processing tax (judged an unconstitutional expropriation of money from one group to benefit another) threw administration fiscal calculations into disarray. To make good a projected revenue shortfall of $620 million, Roosevelt secured passage of a new tax on undistributed corporate profits. This was followed by the Revenue Act of 1937 which clamped down on business tax dodges.

The yield from individual and corporate taxes rose from 27 percent of total federal revenues in FY 1934 to 39 percent in FY 1937–1938, but this was mainly due to economic recovery. Tax reform did little to generate revenue or redistribute wealth. The only real money-maker was the undistributed profits tax. Payroll taxes raised as much each month as the individual income tax provisions of the 1935 Revenue Act did in a year. Only one man in the country, John D. Rockefeller, was subject to the new top rate. Meanwhile, the distribution of wealth remained more or less static. The income share of the poorest 40 percent of families rose only from 12.5 percent in 1929 to 13.6 percent in 1941, which was scarcely larger than the share of the richest 1 percent.

Since fewer than 10 percent of families earned over $3,000

a year and only 1 percent earned over $10,000, raising taxes on the highest incomes was not an effective means to raise revenue or redistribute wealth. What was needed to achieve these aims was a lowering of tax exemption levels in order to widen the tax base and bring the middle classes within its scope. But with few exceptions, such as Robert La Follette, politicians of the 1930s would not countenance this—not even radicals, who preferred to pursue the fiscal red herring of trying to squeeze extra tax payments from millionaires. The middle classes had made plain their resentment about paying high taxes in the Depression. The early 1930s witnessed a citizens' revolt against local property taxes quite as powerful as the rebellion of the late 1970s sparked off by California's Proposition 13 against state taxes. Neither the Roosevelt administration nor Congress wished to bring down such wrath on their heads by subjecting middle-class voters to the federal income tax.

In the words of historian Mark Leff, New Deal tax reform was "one part revenue, two parts rhetoric." It had more significance as political symbolism than fiscal substance. Roosevelt's initiatives undercut the appeal of Huey Long's share-the-wealth movement on the left, and their alienation of the right allowed him to assail "economic royalists," the forces of wealth and privilege, to good effect in his 1936 reelection campaign. Tax reform also replaced deficit spending as the target for business attacks on the New Deal. Corporate leaders charged that its discouragement of investment was responsible for the recession of 1937–1938. Congressional conservatives responded by eliminating the graduated corporate income tax in 1938 and the undistributed profits tax in 1939. It could be argued, however, that the right's assault on these largely symbolic reforms channeled its attentions away from more substantial New Deal programs, such as emergency relief and labor law reform. Tax revision tilted at windmills. Its revenue effects were as limited as those of tax reform, and its agenda was soon overtaken by the coming of war.

## THE CRUCIBLE OF WAR

World War II had a far greater impact on the federal budget than the rather hesitant changes introduced by the New Deal. Outlays totaled $367 billion in FY 1941–1946, nearly double the aggregate amount in the previous century and a half. During the peak years of war production (FY 1943–1945), federal spending amounted to 44.5 percent of GNP, more than double what it had been in World War I. Tax receipts also yielded a massive bounty of $176 billion in FY 1941–1946, but this was nowhere near enough to finance the war effort. The annual deficit averaged $32 billion in this period (17 percent of mean yearly GNP), reaching a high of $54.6 billion (31 percent of GNP) in FY 1943. This dwarfed the New Deal deficits. The gross national debt increased by 450 percent in the war years compared with 165 percent in the Depression decade.

World War II profoundly altered the defense budget. America's retreat from global power in the interwar era was reflected in its relatively low military spending. Defense accounted for about a fifth of federal outlays in FY 1923–1929 and never exceeded $700 million in any year. Its significance declined still further in the 1930s, partly because of the domestic focus of Depression-era budgets but also because of growing isolationist sentiment in Congress and the nation. Military outlays fell from 22 percent ($734 million) of the budget in FY 1930 to 8 percent ($540 million) in FY 1934. In spite of growing international tensions, there was only partial recovery from this low point during the remainder of the decade. In FY 1939 defense spending stood at just over $1 billion, the highest dollar amount since World War I, but its share of the federal budget remained well below the 1920s level. The outbreak of war in Europe in 1939 provided the initial impetus for military expansion, and U.S. entry into the global conflict in 1941 completed the transformation. National defense expenditures rose each year from $6.4 billion in FY 1941 (17.5 percent of outlays) to nearly $83 billion (89.5 percent of outlays) in FY 1945.

The scale of wartime military spending generated no political controversy. Politicians and the public accepted it as necessary to win the war. They also recognized that the defense budget could never return to prewar levels after the war ended. Involvement in World War II had forged a new internationalist consensus. Isolationist sentiment, which had made U.S. entry into the war both reluctant and late, gave way to a new recognition that America's national interests and her responsibilities as a military-economic superpower required active involvement in world affairs. Defense continued to dominate the budget in the postwar era, accounting for about half of total federal outlays between 1945 and 1965.

Wartime disputes over spending centered on domestic rather than defense programs. Mushrooming military costs provided a new rationale for conservative assaults on the New Deal. As a *New Republic* columnist observed, "The plausible argument that the nation cannot afford to buy both guns and social security is all the Roosevelt-baiters have left and they are making the most of it." Relief agencies were particularly vulnerable to the economy drive because wartime full employment had undermined their purpose. The conservative coalition in Congress secured the dissolution of the WPA, the CCC, and the National Youth Administration in 1943. It visited the same fate on the National Resources

Planning Board, cut spending on social programs, and thwarted liberal efforts to revise Social Security. Nevertheless, the conservative attack did not extend to measures that benefited powerful client groups. Instead of disappearing with the return of prosperity, the farm program created in the 1930s was consolidated during the war. There was also bipartisan support for the so-called GI Bill of Rights of 1944, which committed the federal government to a substantial outlay of funds to assist World War II veterans.

Financing the war necessitated major changes in tax policy. Aggregate tax receipts amounted to 48 percent of outlays in FY 1941–1946, compared with 30 percent in World War I. The principal money-makers were individual and corporate income taxes. These generated 65 percent of total revenue in FY 1941–1946, more than double their share in FY 1940. In fact, as historian John Witte noted, FY 1944 and FY 1945 stand out as "the most progressive tax years in U.S. history." Individual and corporate income taxes produced 78 percent of federal revenues in these two years, their respective shares amounting to 43 percent and 35 percent. In no other year since World War II have these taxes contributed a higher percentage of receipts. Indeed, their share declined steadily over the next half-century. In FY 1990 it stood at only 54 percent, largely because corporate income taxes yielded a mere 9 percent of total revenues.

The huge wartime increase in personal tax receipts was due to the expansion of the tax base and wartime prosperity. Early in the war Treasury Secretary Morgenthau observed that "for the first time in our history, the income tax is becoming a people's tax." No more than 5 percent of families had paid individual income taxes in any year during the 1930s, but 74 percent did so in FY 1945. This tax had been transformed from a symbol of wealth to an obligation of citizenship. Massive revenue requirements, the need to restrain consumer demand in the inflation-prone war economy, and the ethos of shared sacrifice to support the war effort established an unanswerable case for restructuring the personal tax system. Wartime prosperity also blunted public resentment of higher taxes because most people were now earning more, even after tax deductions, than in the depressed 1930s.

The Revenue Act of 1942 launched wartime tax reform. It brought most Americans within the tax system by lowering personal exemptions, increased marginal tax rates on individual incomes, raised corporate taxes, and tightened the excess profits tax to ensure that business could not make undue profit from the war. Shortly afterward the Current Tax Payment Act of 1943 introduced the withholding system that remains in operation today. Personal tax was henceforth deducted from paychecks; previously taxpayers had been billed in quarterly installments in the year after the income was earned. The new system eliminated the lag between public expenditure and tax collection, thereby easing government borrowing requirements, and made taxation a more useful antiinflation device because rate increases could be imposed immediately.

In spite of wartime exigencies, tax reform was not free from the kinds of political disputes it had aroused in the late 1930s. Congress was still reluctant to impose stiff tax increases on the middle class and did not give Roosevelt all he asked for in this regard. Influenced by the conservative coalition, it also forced the administration to accept a one-time forgiveness of 1942 tax liabilities, so that rich taxpayers did not face a double levy when the system of immediate tax deductions was introduced in 1943. Roosevelt's continuing efforts to soak the rich in the cause of making the war burden more equitable did not get very far. Congress balked at his proposals in 1942 and 1943 to tax away all annual income above $25,000 ($50,000 for families). Presidential-legislative relations over taxation reached their lowest ebb in early 1944 when Roosevelt vetoed a revenue bill strewn with business loopholes. With its eye on forthcoming elections, Congress responded by overriding a presidential veto of tax legislation for the first time ever.

Political constraints on tax reform contributed to the colossal scale of wartime deficits. The United States funded a smaller proportion of its war effort from taxes than either Britain or Canada. It could easily have borne a higher tax burden, which would have reduced the rate of public debt expansion and eased inflationary pressures. Instead the government had to rely on borrowing. To ensure that deficits could be financed as cheaply as possible, the Treasury wanted interest rates held at their low Depression-era levels. It persuaded the Federal Reserve to subordinate monetary policy to fiscal priorities by buying or selling government securities at officially agreed prices and yields. This "pegging" policy kept interest rates steady and increased the liquidity of U.S. bonds. To raise money the Treasury floated seven War Loans and one Victory Loan. Commercial banks and Federal Reserve banks together purchased 38 percent of government securities issued in FY 1941–1946, but the next most important investor group were individual citizens, who accounted for 25 percent. As a result, the arsenal of democracy never ran out of money.

The massively higher receipts from taxation bore testimony that a depressed economy had been transformed into a booming one during the war. GNP rose by 56 percent in real terms from 1941 to 1945, and unemployment among the civilian labor force fell beneath 2 percent in 1943–1945.

Monetary factors provided the initial impetus for economic expansion. Political turmoil caused a flight of gold from Europe to America in the late 1930s. The inflow continued from Britain (and to a lesser extent France) to pay for war materiel in 1939–1941. These developments resulted in a marked expansion of the money supply, which was sustained by the easy-money policy that the Federal Reserve pursued at the Treasury's behest. But it was the effects of fiscal policy that carried the war boom to new heights. Massive federal spending and the enormous budget deficits spurred the military economy and produced multiplier effects on the civilian economy, resulting in rising productivity, increased employment, and improved living standards.

Wartime economic success provided a substantial boost for the fiscal revolution initiated in the late 1930s. It seemingly offered proof that Keynesian measures could generate prosperity. By 1945 there was widespread acceptance among the nation's political elites on two issues that had aroused controversy in the New Deal era, namely, that government had a responsibility to prevent the return of mass unemployment in peacetime, and that fiscal activism was essential to fulfill this duty. Roosevelt now embraced these principles more frankly and enthusiastically than in the late 1930s. His Republican opponent in the 1944 presidential election, Thomas E. Dewey, was similarly forthright in advocating the need for government action to sustain postwar prosperity. Even the business community began to break ranks. Most corporate leaders continued to avow free-market principles, but the realization that high employment was good for profits induced a change of heart in others. This new outlook was signified by the creation in 1942 of the Committee for Economic Development (CED) to formulate ideas for achieving postwar prosperity through business-government cooperation.

But advocates of fiscal activism held differing views about what it should entail. Business Keynesians, as represented by the CED, believed that government should promote high employment rather than ensure actual full employment. They envisaged the use of fiscal policy to modify fluctuations in the business cycle, mainly through reliance on the automatic, built-in flexibility of the recently expanded income tax. Business Keynesians saw two great advantages to this countercyclical strategy. First, taxation could be used as either an antiinflationary or antideflationary device. Second, balanced budgets would continue as the operative guide of fiscal policy in conditions of economic prosperity.

In contrast, New Deal liberals sought to use government spending powers to guarantee what amounted to full employment, that everybody who wanted a job should have one. The war had dispelled their "stagnationist" theories about the "mature economy" and revived their faith in American capitalism. New Deal liberals were now concerned about how to sustain abundance rather than how to live within economic limits. Wartime experience convinced them that the solution lay in Keynesian policy to boost consumption and economic growth rather than in government regulation of capitalism. In the new liberal credo, economic growth was the surest means of achieving social progress. Indeed, the fiscal and welfare functions of the state were seen as intertwined, because social welfare programs helped to distribute income and boost purchasing power. Guided by the Keynesian economists who had come to Washington to serve in government during the war, notably Alvin Hansen of Harvard University, the New Dealers came to believe that fiscal policy should be determined by continuous analysis and forecast of the amount of federal spending necessary to sustain full employment. The function of the budget in this growth-oriented Keynesianism was to fine-tune the economy. Whether federal finances were balanced or not was irrelevant.

Concerned above all with the duties of commander-in-chief and the foundations of a new postwar international order, Roosevelt paid little heed to the wartime debate over fiscal policy. Whether he could have fully embraced the liberal prescription had he lived to complete his fourth term is unclear. It was the countercyclical fiscal strategy that emerged triumphant in the postwar years. But the growth-oriented Keynesianism that emerged during World War II ultimately found expression in the new economics pursued by the Democratic presidential administrations of the 1960s.

# 3

# The Age of Equilibrium, 1945–1960

THE POSTWAR ERA was an age of equilibrium in budgetary policy. The Democratic administration of Harry S. Truman and the Republican administration of Dwight D. Eisenhower sustained a balance between competing priorities. They upheld traditional balanced-budget ideals but also accepted the modern doctrine that deficit spending was sometimes necessary. Seven of fifteen budgets were in the black between FY 1947 and FY 1961, making this the last time in American history that balanced budgets were achieved with any regularity. Though the scale of postwar spending dwarfed that of the 1930s, the buoyancy of tax revenues kept federal income abreast of outlays. Both Truman and Eisenhower took considerable political risks to keep taxes at a level that would pay for spending. As cold war pressures mounted, they also strove to ensure that the defense budget was kept within limits that the nation could afford. Nor was domestic spending neglected; the postwar era saw the consolidation of many New Deal programs. Finally, both Truman and Eisenhower used fiscal policy to sustain prosperity, but their management of the postwar economy struck a balance between expansionary measures to promote growth and restrictive measures to combat inflation.

## BALANCING THE BUDGET

Federal spending increased sharply in the postwar years, from $34.5 billion (15.4 percent of GNP) in FY 1947 to $97.7 billion (18.9 percent of GNP) in FY 1961. Outlays were 165 percent higher in constant dollar terms in FY 1950 than in FY 1940, and 61 percent higher in FY 1961 than in FY 1950. This rise in expenditure occurred at a time when the budget was usually in or near balance and tax rates were relatively stable. During the Truman presidency the budget was balanced in FY 1947, 1948, 1949, and 1951; the deficits incurred in FY 1950, 1952, and 1953 averaged only 1.1 percent of GNP. During the Eisenhower presidency the budget was balanced in FY 1956, 1957, and 1960, and the deficits in FY 1954, 1955, 1958, 1959, and 1961 averaged just 1 percent of GNP. The U.S. government was in the happy position of being able to spend more without a corollary increase either in taxation or borrowing. It enjoyed the fiscal dividend of incremental revenues produced by an expanding economy. Annual federal income from taxes averaged 17.4 percent of GNP from FY 1947 through FY 1961. Receipts totaled $94.4 billion in FY 1961, nearly six times higher in real terms than in FY 1940.

Instead of falling back into depression, as many Americans had feared, the economy enjoyed a long boom after World War II. Demobilization brought a temporary downturn, but the subsequent expansion was swift and durable. Real GNP surpassed its wartime peak in 1950 and stood at more than double its 1940 level by 1960. Annual economic growth during the 1950s averaged 3.3 percent. With only 6 percent of the world's population, the United States produced and consumed over 25 percent of total world goods and services in 1960. This growth was accompanied by high employment, low inflation, and rising wage levels. In the 1950s the jobless rate averaged just 4.4 percent, and the consumer price index rose by only 2.1 percent a year. By 1960 the real income of the average American was 35 percent higher than in 1945.

Postwar economic growth had several sources. The United States enjoyed a dominant position in world trade because the economies of its main industrial competitors had been ravaged by the war. Consumer demand was strong, as Americans were able at last to spend the money they had saved during the war when goods were scarce. Credit was also cheap, particularly in the late 1940s. The construction and automobile industries enjoyed spectacular growth because of demand for new homes and cars. New industries boosted by the war, notably electronics, plastics, and chemicals, also experienced rapid growth. Thanks to increased investment by business, postwar prosperity owed far more to productivity gains than had been the case in the past, when population expansion had been the main source of economic growth. Another novel stimulant was government spending. The public sector did not shrink back to its pre–New Deal size with the advent of peace and prosperity. In 1955 government (federal, state, and local combined) was responsible for one-fifth of total purchases in the private sector, making it by far the largest buyer, and overall public spending accounted for 25 percent of GNP, compared with 10 percent in 1929.

Prosperity was not a guarantee of balanced budgets, as post-1960 history would show. Political leadership was also instrumental in shaping postwar fiscal history. Even though Republicans demonized Harry Truman as a reckless spender, he believed that the budget should be balanced other than in times of national emergency or recession. As he remarked in his memoirs, "There is nothing sacred about the pay-as-

you-go idea so far as I am concerned except that it represents
the soundest principle of financing that I know." Though he
had served the New Deal loyally as a Missouri senator
before being drafted as Franklin D. Roosevelt's running
mate in 1944, Truman had not participated in the great
debates over Keynesianism. His fiscal convictions were based
not on economic theory but on his instincts and experience.
Having suffered personal business failure in the brief
economic downturn that followed World War I, Truman
believed that government had a duty to counteract recession.
On the other hand, his experience in his first political office,
that of a county administrator in the 1920s and early 1930s,
convinced him that government also had a responsibility to
uphold fiscal discipline and give value in its use of public
funds.

Truman operated three balanced budgets in his first term
but only one in his second term, when the intensification of
the cold war caused a huge increase in military outlays.
Eisenhower, the first Republican president in twenty years,
was determined to halt the revival of deficit spending.
Though he balanced the budget only three times, this was
arguably a more impressive record than Truman's because
military costs throughout the 1950s were far higher than in
the late 1940s. Without doubt Eisenhower evinced greater
determination to balance the budget than any president from
the 1930s to the present. As he affirmed in 1958, "I think
nothing is more necessary in our domestic affairs than to
examine, each day, our economy, as well as our government
receipts and expenditures, and to act prudently."

Formerly wartime commander of U.S. and Allied forces
in Europe, Eisenhower had no background in party politics
before running for president in 1952, but he had a well-
defined philosophy of political economy. As a pragmatic

conservative, he saw balanced budgets as a means to constrain big government. Above all, he feared that deficit spending during prosperity would fuel inflation. Eisenhower's views were similar to those of the business leaders associated with the Committee for Economic Development, many of whom had promoted his presidential candidacy. Their common line of reasoning went as follows. Deficits, though necessary in recession, resulted at other times in excessive demand for goods and services. The pressure that this put on scarce resources would nominally increase GNP—but with little capacity for output to expand; the real result would be to bid up prices. Also, increased government borrowing would compete with private demand for credit, which was always high during prosperity, therefore making interest-rate hikes inevitable. Inflation, in Eisenhower's view, was the bane of modern society, because it created conflict between labor, business, and consumers, discouraged thrift and saving, and undermined business confidence. His main fear was that its progressive erosion of the dollar's value would undermine America's capacity to wage the cold war. "We can only combat communism in the long term if our economy is healthy," he warned in 1953.

Both Truman and Eisenhower took political risks to preserve the fiscal dividend of high revenues, the essential foundation of postwar budget balancing. In contrast to the period after World War I, there was no major reduction in wartime tax levels between 1945 and 1960. The basic progressivity of the taxation system established in World War II was also sustained. Corporate income taxes provided 26 percent of federal revenues in FY 1947–1961. Individual income taxes yielded a larger share of 43 percent, reflecting the rise in wage levels and the expansion of the labor force in the booming economy.

The Truman administration initially sponsored modest tax cuts to ease the problems of postwar economic reconversion. With outlays down by two-thirds since 1945, however, it was able to achieve a budget surplus in FY 1948 of $11.8 billion (4.8 percent of GNP and equivalent to $76 billion in 1987 dollars), the largest in history. Truman's willingness to cut taxes soon gave way to concerns about inflation and debt reduction. But Republicans, who won control of Congress in 1946, wanted further tax reduction as an incentive for capital investment and to force cutbacks in domestic spending. In 1947 they twice enacted tax cuts weighted toward upper-income groups but narrowly failed to override Truman's veto of each bill. Bowing to election-year pressures, the president issued his own tax reduction proposal in 1948 (a cost-of-living credit for each taxpayer and dependent) that was to be financed through an increase in corporate taxes. Republicans countered with a new measure combining benefits for lower-income earners with supply-side incentives for business and high earners. This was carried over the president's veto but yielded a feeble political harvest. In his "give-'em-hell" reelection campaign, Truman castigated the GOP for fiscal irresponsibility and lack of social justice in promoting what he portrayed as a rich-man's tax bill. What part this played in his surprise victory is unclear, but his tactics created doubt about the political advantages of tax cuts. Accordingly, he faced less pressure on this score during his second term.

America's involvement in the Korean War from 1950 to 1953 presented new fiscal challenges. Truman's budgetary policy during this conflict spared the nation from the kind of inflationary problems that later resulted from Lyndon Johnson's financial mismanagement of the Vietnam War. His experience as chairman of the Senate special committee that investigated the national defense program in World War

II stood him in good stead. Truman was convinced that wartime taxes should have been higher. In his opinion, Roosevelt's reliance on borrowing to pay for the war had caused an unnecessary expansion of the national debt and had fueled inflationary pressures that were unleashed once wartime controls were removed. There was only one sensible way to finance the Korean War, Truman told the American people: "It is the plain, simple, direct way. We should pay...as we go out of taxes."

Truman got three revenue bills through Congress in 1950–1951. These restored relative tax levels close to those of World War II. Among other things, they provided for temporary increases in personal and corporate income tax rates, a new excess profits tax, and excise tax increases. But the president found growing resistance among conservative congressmen from both parties, who preferred to balance the budget through spending cuts rather than tax increases. The Revenue Act of 1951 provided only half the $10 billion tax increase Truman wanted. His 1952 proposal to close business tax loopholes, notably the oil depletion allowance, was summarily rejected. The Korean War tax increases did not keep federal finances in the black, but they helped to contain the deficit within manageable proportions during a period when the military budget swelled. The incremental revenue benefits of an economy enjoying a strong wartime boom also facilitated the task of budget control. In total, receipts mushroomed from $39.4 billion (14.8 percent of GNP) in FY 1950 to $66.2 billion (19.3 percent of GNP) in FY 1952.

Republican hopes that Eisenhower would substantially reduce the tax burden were doomed to disappointment. Budget receipts were 18.3 percent of GNP in FY 1960, only slightly below the Korean War level and well above the average of 16 percent in the late 1940s. Moreover, individual income tax receipts were 10.4 percent of aggregate personal income in FY 1960, compared with 7.7 percent in FY 1950. Eisenhower was reluctant to cut taxes until he could halt the upward trend of spending and balance the budget on a regular basis, which he was never able to do.

The Republican administration's major initiative in tax policy was the tax reform of 1954, which completely rewrote and modernized the federal income tax code but provided only minimal tax reduction in the form of more generous allowances for business and individuals. Eisenhower resisted Democratic calls for an increase in the exemption level on personal income, which would have freed millions of low-income families from their income tax liability. Reaffirming the wartime view that this tax had become a mark of citizenship, he avowed, "Every real American is proud to carry his share of the burden." In response, Democrats charged that tax reform had become a giveaway to the rich, reminiscent of the "trickle down" policies of the 1920s. This was hardly the case, since the 1954 measure left in place not only very high marginal rates but also the revenue base to support increased spending.

Eisenhower fought hard against tax reduction. To prevent a large deficit in FY 1954, he persuaded congressional Republicans to support a six-month extension of the personal income tax surcharges and the excess profits tax that had been levied as temporary measures to fund the Korean War. In the interests of party unity, Eisenhower did accept a selective reduction of excise rates in 1954, but he periodically persuaded Congress to approve extension bills that kept corporate tax rates and some excises at their Korean War levels for the remainder of his presidency. Tax policy also occasioned dispute within the administration itself. In 1955 and again in 1956 Treasury Secretary George Humphrey pleaded for an investment-boosting tax cut to be awarded before the budget was in balance, arguing that the resultant economic expansion would generate enough additional revenues for the deficit to be eliminated. Yet Eisenhower remained adamant that no tax reduction would be funded from a deficit "as long as I'm here." During the recessions of 1954 and 1958, Democrats also mounted strong pressure for a consumption-boosting tax cut aimed at lower-income groups. Eisenhower had no qualms about holding his ground in 1954, when the downturn was relatively moderate, but the severity of the second recession made him think hard about a temporary reduction of taxes. In the end he desisted for fear that Congress would find it politically impossible to raise taxes when the economy recovered.

Eisenhower resisted the political temptation to cut taxes in the election years of 1954, 1956, and 1958. In the last case his stand hurt his party because it prolonged the 1958 recession. GOP leaders, especially Vice-President Richard Nixon, wanted Eisenhower to make up for this by cutting taxes before the 1960 elections. The balancing of the FY 1960 budget seemingly created a platform for such action. But Eisenhower was adamant that tax reduction should be deferred until several national debt-reducing surpluses had been achieved. "Once we have established such payments as normal practice," he declared in his last State of the Union Address, "we can profitably make improvements in our tax structure and thereby truly reduce the heavy burdens of taxation."

## Uncle Sam's Leviathan

During the cold war era the United States undertook a huge military buildup. Both Truman and Eisenhower sought to ensure that this development did not compromise balanced-budget goals. By and large the defense budgetary process was dominated by the president in this period. This reflected a consensus on cold war aims and congressional recognition that the executive branch had superior expertise and resources to assess defense requirements. Presidential supremacy facilitated expenditure control. As political scientist Dennis Ippolito observed, "For defense, top-down budgeting was essential in order to reconcile national security needs with what the economy and the budget could bear."

Congress usually went along with the president's estimate of how much defense the nation could afford. It often disputed funding levels for one of the armed services or a particular military program but rarely challenged the overall expenditure recommendation. In other words, Congress would reallocate money within the military budget but not substantially alter the total appropriation. This was largely a depoliticized process in which the main players were not the party leaders but the defense experts on the armed services committees and defense appropriations subcommittees in both houses. The few serious challenges to overall estimates were made chiefly in the cause of economy rather than expansion. Congressional Republicans were desperately anxious to slash military spending after the Korean War in order to finance tax reduction within a balanced budget. The GOP-controlled Eighty-third Congress reduced Eisenhower's defense estimates by 3.9 percent for FY 1954 and 3.6 percent for FY 1955. He fared much better when the legislature was controlled by the Democrats, who accepted the need for large military appropriations. From FY 1956 through FY 1961, congressional amendments to presidential defense estimates amounted to a net cut of only .5 percent in total funding.

The Truman Doctrine of 1947 promulgated a containment

strategy to counter Soviet expansionism. Initially Truman estimated that the nation could afford defense spending of $12 billion to $14 billion a year in pursuit of cold war aims. He shared the widespread belief that if peacetime military outlays exceeded $15 billion, the consequent surge in inflation would demand the introduction of wage and price controls. Another popular theory held that the Soviet Union was trying to scare the United States into spending so much on defense that it would bankrupt itself. At this juncture the president and his advisers were confident that America's monopoly of the atomic bomb ensured its security against Soviet attack. Their main fear was that communism would expand through political means. Hence they were more intent on helping to reconstruct the war-torn economies of vulnerable European nations and of Nationalist China than on building up military power. This also benefited U.S. industry since recipients of foreign aid were expected to buy American goods in return. Outlays on programs like the Marshall Plan averaged nearly two-fifths of defense spending in FY 1947–1949. Almost the only group to complain that the military budget was inadequate was the military itself. Truman resisted determined pressure from the armed services, particularly the air force, for a huge expansion of funds that would have put the budgets of FY 1949 and 1950 deep in the red.

Before long, however, Truman himself came to believe that far more had to be spent on defense. Two unexpected developments in 1949—the Soviet attainment of atomic capability and the Communist overthrow of the Nationalist regime in China—compelled a reassessment of America's security requirements. In 1950 State and Defense department officials collaborated to produce a top-secret report known as NSC-68. This was the blueprint for the globalization and militarization of containment. NSC-68 called for the Truman Doctrine, hitherto applied only in Europe, to be extended worldwide. It warned that the Soviet Union was developing "the military capacity to support its design for world domination" and would have the nuclear capability to destroy the United States by 1954, deemed the "year of maximum danger." In these circumstances America could no longer ask how much security it could afford, nor could it distinguish between global and national security.

NSC-68 recommended that the United States rebuild its military power in order to meet the Soviets at every level of conflict, conventional or atomic, global or limited. This would necessitate spending $40 billion or more on defense each year for the foreseeable future. Military outlays of this magnitude had been considered economically ruinous, but NSC-68 employed the rationale of military Keynesianism to discount such fears. While accepting that budget deficits were inevitable, it cited the experience of World War II as evidence that the expanded defense program could boost GNP and produce a real improvement in the nation's standard of living.

The outbreak of war in Korea was the catalyst for the implementation of NSC-68. While pursuing a limited-war strategy against the Soviet Union's clients in East Asia, the Truman administration prepared to fight a global war in anticipation of a possible direct attack by the Soviets on the U.S. and its allies in 1954. By FY 1953 total national security outlays on the armed services, military foreign aid, and atomic energy amounted to $52.8 billion (14.4 percent of GNP), compared with $13.7 billion (5.1 percent of GNP) in FY 1950. This rapid buildup was not devoted exclusively to the Korean conflict. It also financed huge increases in air power, atomic weapons development (a hydrogen device was successfully tested in late 1952), and conventional force expansion, notably of U.S. ground troops stationed in Western Europe.

Truman's successor viewed this defense expansion with dismay. Eisenhower, the former professional soldier, had a keen sense of the economic limits of U.S. military power. He thought the accelerated defense buildup to meet a possible Soviet attack in the year of maximum danger was misguided. "We're not in a moment of danger," he warned, "we're in an age of danger." The time of attack could not be reliably predicted, and if American forecasts proved incorrect, the options of continued military expansion or substantial cutbacks were equally unacceptable. In contrast to the authors of NSC-68, Eisenhower feared that unrestrained military spending would hurt not help the economy. In his view it could only lead to the introduction of economic controls to keep inflationary pressures in check and channel national resources into defense. To Eisenhower, the development of a cold war garrison state posed almost as much danger to the American way of life as communism itself. Accordingly, he advocated a steady defense buildup based on what the nation needed and could afford as the only solution to what he termed the "Great Equation"—"how to equate needed military strength with maximum economic strength."

Eisenhower was determined not to squander the peace dividend made possible by the ending of the Korean War in mid-1953. Shortly afterward the new administration's defense reassessment was embodied in the NSC-162/2 report, which became the basis for the so-called New Look strategy. This did not change America's national security goals, only the means of achieving them. Containment policy was sustained, but greater reliance was placed on developing nuclear superiority to curb Communist expansion. It was assumed that this would deter the Soviets and their allies from major acts of aggression, thereby preventing land wars like Korea. Massive short-term military expansion based on a target date was replaced by a steady "long-haul" buildup of air-atomic power and cutbacks in conventional defense. Thanks to the New Look, the air force, which had the smallest of the service budgets in FY 1950, received as many funds in FY 1960 as the army and navy combined. Worst affected was the army, which was scheduled to lose one-third of its personnel. Eisenhower avowed that the new program would achieve "effectiveness with economy," but the alliterative slogan popularized by the media was "more bang for the buck."

Without doubt, budgetary considerations were initially as important as security factors in shaping this policy. The substitution of technology for manpower was cost-effective. Although the need for ever more sophisticated missiles would eventually prove a massive burden on the budget, nuclear weapons were considerably cheaper than conventional forces in the 1950s. It was initially estimated that the New Look would permit defense spending to be reduced to a plateau of $33 billion to $34 billion by the end of Eisenhower's first term, which would allow a balanced budget. Rapid progress was made toward this goal. Total national security expenditure was reduced by nearly one-fifth from FY 1953 through FY 1955, and defense cutbacks accounted for over 80 percent of this retrenchment. Nevertheless, Eisenhower soon felt compelled to modify the New Look in response to Soviet strategic advances.

The NSC-68 rearmament program had briefly given the U.S. nuclear superiority over the Soviets. From 1956 onward, however, there existed a balance of terror in which both sides had the capability to destroy the other. Because nuclear war was now unthinkable, American air-atomic power was less credible as a deterrent against Communist aggression in local and regional crises. Eisenhower recognized the need to compensate for this. The original New Look assumed U.S. strategic superiority and conventional force inferiority. The revised New Look envisaged "superiority" in neither but "sufficiency" in both. In other words, America had to ensure not only that its retaliatory capacity was strong enough to deter a Soviet nuclear strike but also that its conventional forces were adequate to deal with small-war situations. As a result it became much more difficult to keep the lid on defense spending.

Eisenhower's efforts to balance the needs of defense and of the economy encountered contrary pressures during his first term. The Republican right was dissatisfied with the pace of military retrenchment. Within the cabinet, conservatives like Treasury Secretary Humphrey were also anxious for "meat ax" cuts in defense to finance tax reduction. Meanwhile, Eisenhower faced criticism from the military, particularly the army, that his cutbacks had undermined national security. Many Democrats also charged that he was sacrificing defense needs to the priorities of a balanced budget. Some accused him of surrendering air-atomic superiority. Others berated him for depriving U.S. military strategy of flexibility by overdependence on nuclear capability. Nevertheless, Eisenhower was a president uniquely equipped to decide how much security was enough. Sustained by his certainty that he was doing the right thing and by the public's confidence in his experience, he was able to resist the demands of both the economizers and the expansionists.

Controversy over defense spending intensified after the Soviet launch of the Sputnik satellites into space orbit in late 1957. These technological triumphs shattered American illusions of scientific supremacy and aroused fears that the

Soviets now possessed the rocket technology to launch an intercontinental missile attack on the United States. Eisenhower faced criticism from Democrats, defense experts, and some Republicans, all of whom claimed that his penny-pinching had allowed the Soviets to gain the lead in space and missile technology. The chorus grew louder after portions of the Gaither Commission report were leaked. This secret study of deterrence, commissioned by the president, estimated that annual defense appropriations of $48 billion were needed to ensure national security, and recommended an accelerated five-year program of missile, strategic bomber, and fallout-shelter development to restore U.S. nuclear superiority. This would necessitate a series of unbalanced budgets, but the Gaither report, like NSC-68, professed confidence that military Keynesianism would benefit the economy. A Rocke-feller Brothers Fund committee, chaired by Henry Kissinger, reached similar conclusions.

Eisenhower's own economic advisers expressed grave doubts about the inflationary effects of military deficits, reinforcing his fears about a garrison state. He was also well aware that Soviet rocket technology was crude and far inferior to America's B-52 planes as a means of nuclear bomb delivery. Secret intelligence from the U-2 spy flights later revealed that the Soviets possessed relatively few missiles. All this persuaded Eisenhower to hold the line. He requested extra defense appropriations to ease public concern, but rejected a big expansion. Though Congress voted higher funding than he wanted in FY 1959 and FY 1961, the increases were not huge. Eisenhower refused to spend some of this money, citing his authority as commander-in-chief to impound wasteful appropriations. Sputnik's fiscal impact was therefore limited. The FY 1960 military budget breached the sym-bolically important $40 billion mark recommended by

NSC-68, but this was actually the lowest level of defense spending in real terms since FY 1951. As historian Stephen Ambrose noted, Eisenhower's refusal to be panicked by Sputnik "saved his country untold billions of dollars and no one knows how many war scares.... [This] may have been his finest gift to the nation, if only because he was the only man who could have given it."

Despite winning the battle of the budget over Sputnik, Eisenhower fared less well in the ongoing war of words. As the 1960 presidential election approached, Democrats grew insistent that the U.S. was vulnerable to attack because the defense budget was inadequate. Presidential candidate Senator John F. Kennedy of Massachusetts told the nation that it faced a choice about "which gamble ... we take, our money or our survival." If elected he promised extra funding to eliminate the so-called missile gap and to enhance America's conventional forces to meet the growing Communist challenge in the developing world. The collapse of the Paris "peace summit" in mid-1960, which killed hopes of détente with the Soviets, added weight to these attacks. Even Republican presidential candidate, Richard Nixon, in pledging to loosen the military purse strings if he won office, implied dissatisfaction with Eisenhower's policy. The election therefore provided a mandate for defense expansion under a new administration. Eisenhower made one last effort to preserve his legacy. In his stirring Farewell Address of January 1961 he again warned the nation about the folly of excessive defense expenditure and the need to control what he called "the military-industrial complex." Every proposal for increased funding, he avowed, "must be weighed in the light of ... the need to maintain balance ... between the cost and the hoped-for advantage."

## CONSOLIDATING THE NEW DEAL

Harry Truman's unexpected reelection in 1948 signified that the New Deal would remain an integral element in the postwar political consensus. Over the next twelve years both he and Eisenhower built upon Roosevelt's legacy. Truman's efforts to launch a program of new reforms known as the Fair Deal were largely frustrated by the conservative Democratic-Republican coalition in Congress, but he was successful in expanding programs that traced their pedigree to the New Deal. In private Eisenhower expressed fear that the New Deal had launched the nation along "the kind of road that if followed forever will lead toward socialism." Yet he also realized that it would be politically suicidal for the GOP to try to undo what FDR had created. As president, therefore, he sought to develop a modern Republicanism that assimilated the New Deal legacy but drew the line against expanding federal responsibilities into new areas.

The postwar consolidation of the New Deal had a significant impact on the budget. Domestic spending grew steadily from $12 billion in FY 1947 (5 percent of GNP) to $37 billion in FY 1960 (7 percent of GNP). This was broadly in line with overall budgetary growth. When Eisenhower left office, domestic programs accounted for 40 percent of total outlays, which was comparable with their average share in Truman's first term.

The major expansion in domestic spending occurred in so-called human resource programs, which rose from $10 billion (4.4 percent of GNP) in FY 1947 to $30 billion (5.8 percent of GNP) in FY 1960. By and large these were so-called entitlement programs that were not subject to control through the normal appropriations process. Benefits were paid out to everyone who met eligibility requirements set by law, so program outlays were nondiscretionary. In other words, the federal government had an obligation to make payments without regard to other considerations of budgetary policy.

In the Truman era the largest of these programs was veterans' benefits and services, reflecting the bounty of the GI Bill of 1944 to those who served in World War II. In FY 1956 Social Security became the biggest spender, a status it has held ever since. Its expansion was partly a result of demographic trends as workers who had been paying into the program since Roosevelt's day reached retirement age. It also reflected major improvements in the Social Security system promoted by the Truman and Eisenhower administrations. The occupational categories covered by the program were massively expanded in 1950 and 1954 to include farm workers, domestics, and the self-employed. Benefit coverage was also strengthened in 1956 and 1960 to include the disabled and female early retirees. Social Security taxes were periodically raised to support these developments but remained low in comparison to the post-1977 period. In marked contrast to the present day, they made up a much smaller percentage of total tax receipts than corporation income taxes in FY 1951–1960. The high ratio of program contributors to program beneficiaries ensured that low Social Security taxes were affordable in the postwar era. This happy state of affairs would soon change, necessitating big tax hikes to underwrite the solvency of the Social Security system.

Outlays on noncontributory public assistance programs also rose from $600 million (.3 percent of GNP) in FY 1945 to $3.3 billion (.7 percent of GNP) in FY 1960, but this hardly represented a significant improvement of the welfare system. Piecemeal changes were made in various categorical grant programs to widen eligibility for assistance and, in some instances, to increase the federal share of matching grants to the states. But there was no federal funding for general assistance and very little for government-sponsored employment. Welfare reformers also failed to achieve their major legislative goals: guaranteed minimum subsistence payments for categorical-aid recipients, large-scale public housing, and national health insurance. As a result, poverty remained very much a part of the affluent society, blighting the lives of one in four Americans.

At the same time the growth in spending on physical resource programs from $2 billion (.9 percent of GNP) in FY 1947 to $10.4 billion (2 percent of GNP) in FY 1960 sustained the development of the investor state. In contrast to human resource programs, spending on these programs was controllable through the annual appropriations process and was therefore more responsive to overall budget strategy. The sole exception was agriculture, since price support outlays were determined by farm production levels. Discretionary program funding tended to fluctuate in relationship to other spending pressures and balanced-budget requirements. After a marked expansion in the late 1940s, outlays were held steady in these areas during the defense buildup of the early 1950s and were then reduced as part of Eisenhower's first-term drive to balance the budget. But policy changes and political pressures resulted in sustained growth of physical resource spending in the late 1950s.

The most important development was in transportation. The enactment in 1956 of the interstate highway program launched the biggest public works project in American history. Although the scheme was initially mooted in World War II, its implementation was delayed for a decade because of dispute over its scope and how to pay for it. The big cities feared that urban taxpayers would finance a program advantageous only to suburban and rural areas. Eisenhower, who was personally committed to the project because of its economic benefits and defense applications, helped to break the deadlock. It was eventually agreed to establish a trust fund financed by user fees and fuel taxes. Federal funding was set at 90 percent of costs, whereas previous highway programs had required the states to pay up to half the bill. Interstate program costs proved to be far higher than anticipated, largely because of the expense of building urban freeways through inner cities. Initially these roads had been intended to go around the cities, but the plan was changed to win urban support for the program. Since the enabling legislation required that the highway trust fund never operate a deficit, the extra costs had to be financed through regular increases in highway and gasoline taxes rather than from the general budget.

By contrast, Eisenhower struggled to limit federal responsibility in other areas. Building on New Deal foundations, the Truman administration had significantly expanded spending on multipurpose public water projects. Eisenhower objected to this not only on grounds of cost but also out of preference for private power development and greater state-local involvement in water resource projects. New projects were blocked and spending cutbacks imposed on existing ones during the first two years of his administration. The Democrats reversed this trend after regaining a majority in Congress in 1955. They deemed these programs essential to strengthen the infrastructure of the economy. The fact that many congressmen in both parties also viewed public water projects as an important means of distributing "pork barrel" benefits to their constituencies intensified the pressure for higher spending.

Eisenhower's greatest domestic disappointment was his

failure to reduce the farm program. He considered the system of federal regulation through price supports to be wasteful, extravagant, and ineffective. In his view it benefited only the big commercial farmers, who produced 85 percent of total agricultural output by 1960, and generated crop surpluses through its distortion of supply and demand. The administration achieved some price-support reduction in 1954 and 1956, but rural congressmen from both parties resisted more drastic proposals that would have moved the farm economy closer to the free market. Not only was the farm program costly, it also made budget planning difficult because outlays could swing widely as a result of changing production levels. In FY 1959, for example, farm spending was almost twice as high ($2 billion more) as in the preceding year, but then fell back by the same amount in FY 1960. A frustrated Eisenhower left office regarding the parity system as a disgrace.

## The Management of Prosperity

Franklin D. Roosevelt had belatedly recognized the usefulness of fiscal policy as an economic stimulant in the late 1930s. Truman and Eisenhower also used the budget to manage the economy. Both depended in different ways on the maintenance of American capitalism's well-being to achieve their political goals. Truman regarded economic growth as essential to provide more jobs and better wages and to pay for the expanded costs of government. Eisenhower saw national prosperity as the essential foundation of the cold war state and the best safeguard against the expansion of the New Deal state. In contrast to Roosevelt, however, both their fiscal policies had to balance high-employment concerns with the need to curb inflation in the buoyant postwar economy. Both administrations could claim to have managed the economy successfully. Average unemployment in the postwar era was remarkably low, and excepting the war-affected years of 1946–1947 and 1951–1952, only 1957 could be labeled an inflationary year (using economist Arthur Okun's 1970 definition of this as a year in which both the Consumer Price Index and the GNP deflator—which measures the prices of all newly produced goods and services— rose by 2.75 percent or more).

The framework of the postwar political economy was established by the Employment Act of 1946. Led by Senators James Murray of Montana and Robert Wagner of New York, liberal Democrats produced a draft bill that mandated the federal government to ensure full employment through compensatory spending on public works, education, health care, and other social programs. But it encountered strong opposition from the bipartisan conservative coalition in Congress and business. Some business groups, notably the National Association of Manufacturers, remained implacably hostile to federal intervention in the economy. Others, such as the Committee for Economic Development and the U.S. Chamber of Commerce, were convinced by the experience of depression and war that some degree of economic management by the state was necessary. But they feared that an explicit guarantee of full employment would become a smokescreen for social activism by a liberal administration, resulting either in permanent deficit spending or in increased taxation to pay for domestic program costs. The final bill embodied the concerns of these moderate business groups. Shorn of full-employment and public spending commitments, it merely prescribed a federal obligation "to promote maximum employment, production and purchasing power." As such, the Employment Act represented a victory for the business Keynesianism that had emerged in World War II.

In spite of its limitations, the legislation marked a further stage in the fiscal revolution initiated by the New Deal. It institutionalized federal responsibility for combating recession and rising unemployment. In the absence of a compensatory spending commitment, the so-called automatic stabilizers— the automatic decrease of tax revenues and corollary increase of unemployment insurance payouts in a recession—would serve as the primary instruments to reverse economic decline. Meanwhile, the emphasis on "maximum purchasing power" implied a mandate to curb inflation as well as joblessness. The Employment Act also formalized the president's pre- eminence in economic policymaking requiring him to report to Congress annually on the state of the economy and to recommend whatever measures were necessary to ensure its well-being. To assist him the act created the Council of Economic Advisers (CEA) within the Executive Office of the President. Consisting of three members and a research staff, this body became the bailiwick of professional economists who regarded the budget mainly in terms of its significance for economic stabilization. The CEA acted as a counterpoint to the Treasury, hitherto the president's main source of economic counsel and traditionally an advocate of balanced budgets because of its responsibility for managing the national debt and the international value of the dollar.

The fiscal policy of the Truman and Eisenhower admini- strations was governed by a concern to modify excesses in the business cycle—what the new economists of the 1960s referred to dismissively as a "cyclical mentality." It was accepted that there would be a recurrent pattern of fluctu- ations in economic activity over several years; periods of growth in prices, incomes, employment, and productivity would alternate with periods of recession in which the same variables would decline. Both administrations sought to guard against an excessive downswing that could cause a slump and an excessive upswing which could overheat the economy and generate inflation. In contrast to their successors in the 1960s, neither sought to accelerate the basic rate of economic growth around which cyclical fluctuations occurred.

The recessions of the postwar era were short and shallow, so they did not provide a stern test for fiscal policy. Truman's response to the 1949 downturn provided the first concrete expression of the legitimacy of compensatory deficits under the Employment Act of 1946. As he avowed, "We cannot expect to achieve a budget surplus in a declining economy. There are economic and social deficits that would be far more serious than a temporary deficit in the federal budget." Nevertheless, Truman's main compensatory actions were negative in nature: he abandoned efforts to persuade the newly elected Democratic Congress to rescind the tax cut voted by the previous Republican Congress and resisted demands from the bipartisan conservative coalition to balance the budget through spending cutbacks. The $3.2 billion deficit run up in FY 1950 was due to the automatic stabilizers rather than discretionary measures. This amounted to only 1.2 percent of GNP, a far smaller share than every New Deal deficit except that of FY 1938. It was the underlying strength of the economy rather than the effectiveness of fiscal policy that ensured a swift recovery.

Eisenhower's response to the recession of 1953–1954 was also more important in political than fiscal terms. As the first Republican president since the New Deal, his acceptance of unbalanced budgets strengthened the legitimacy of compensatory deficits. In placing a bipartisan seal of approval on the use of fiscal policy to combat recession, Eisenhower removed the albatross of Hooverism from the GOP's neck.

But he was in the fortunate position of being able to have his budgetary cake and eat it too. Despite a fall in tax receipts, the deficit actually narrowed in the recession-affected FY 1955 budget because post–Korean War military retrenchment caused a rapid decline of outlays. Deficit reduction has never occurred in any other recession from 1945 to the present.

One of the factors that had triggered the 1953–1954 recession was the reduction in federal demand for goods and services resulting from defense cutbacks. Reassured by the CEA that the decline would be mild, Eisenhower refused to authorize compensatory spending increases that might burden the budget for years to come. Tax policy was more expansionary, but the administration deserved little of the credit for this. Total tax reduction in calendar 1954 amounted to $7.4 billion, the largest amount in any single year to date, but $5 billion resulted from the automatic expiration of Korean War taxes and $1 billion came from congressional cuts in excise duties. The administration threw its weight against demands for personal tax reduction to boost consumption. Nevertheless, tax reduction in combination with the operation of the automatic stabilizers and the relaxation of monetary policy helped to sustain aggregate purchasing power during the period of recession. As a result, the administration could claim to have fulfilled its obligations as prescribed by the Employment Act.

In reality both Truman and Eisenhower worried more about inflation than unemployment. This was understandable in Truman's case because he had to deal with the post–World War II inflationary spiral and the price instability generated by the Korean War. Eisenhower's near obsession with an inflation rate that averaged less than 2 percent may be less comprehensible to present-day Americans, particularly those who remember the high inflation of the 1970s. It must be borne in mind that postwar leaders were conditioned by their own experience to regard a zero inflation rate as necessary and attainable. Creeping inflation of 1 to 2 percent a year was unacceptable to Eisenhower and his advisers, who feared that it would produce a serious cumulative devaluation of money if sustained for long. Typifying this view, CEA chairman Raymond Saulnier avowed that in the face of inflationary pressures there was "no viable alternative to a budget policy that is essentially conservative."

Where Truman regarded a balanced budget as the basic safeguard against inflation, Eisenhower went further in actually seeking to reduce federal expenditure. He proclaimed in 1957, "If the budget is too high inflation occurs, which in effect cuts down the value of the dollar, so that nothing is gained and the process is self-defeating." Under Eisenhower, administrative budget outlays (programs financed through the regular appropriations process) were below the previous year's level in FY 1954, 1955, and 1960. Although the overall trend in his presidency was to expand administrative outlays, the fact that spending was reduced in three of his eight budgets stands in marked contrast to the incremental growth of expenditure throughout the 1960s, 1970s, and 1980s.

In addition to fiscal policy, both the Truman and Eisenhower administrations utilized monetary policy to manage the economy. The termination of the wartime "peg" agreement in 1951 freed the Federal Reserve from its obligation to support Treasury borrowing. This allowed it greater flexibility to respond to changing economic circumstances. Timely expansionary measures by the Federal Reserve helped the economy to recover quickly from the three Eisenhower-era recessions, but its main concern was with inflation. Eisenhower found himself relying more and more on the Fed to fight inflation because of his failure to keep the lid on federal spending.

To the Eisenhower administration, price stability was essential for sustainable economic growth. In the late 1950s, however, the Democrats advocated the reverse case—that expanding the economy's productive capacity was the best defense against inflation. This was a logical extension of the Keynesian doctrines that had gained credence among liberals during World War II. With the economy growing rapidly during the Truman era, Democrats had not questioned the need to curb inflation. But the slower growth rate achieved under Eisenhower led them to believe he was sacrificing expanded prosperity to wage war on inflation. The Sputnik crisis intensified their concern that slow growth was responsible for the U.S. falling behind in the arms race because it starved the federal government of extra tax revenues to finance defense expansion. And the recurrence of recessions in 1957–1958 and 1960–1961 seemed to indicate that the main economic problem was inadequate rather than excessive demand.

The Eisenhower administration's cure for the surge of inflation in 1957 was a dose of budgetary retrenchment and monetary restraint, but this helped tip the economy into the most serious recession of the postwar era. While unemployment rose over the five million mark for the first time since 1940 (7 percent of the labor force), inflation did not fall as it usually did in periods of recession. This combination was a foretaste of the stagflation that the economy would suffer in the 1970s. Fear of aggravating inflation deterred Eisenhower from implementing a deficit spending program and tax cuts to boost recovery. The president also locked horns with congressional Democrats, using his veto power to block enactment of their compensatory proposals. Although the FY 1959 budget ran up a deficit of $12.8 billion, in current dollar terms a peacetime record, this represented a smaller percentage of GNP than almost every New Deal deficit. Precious little of the imbalance was attributable to anti-recession activism. The bulk of the deficit resulted from the operation of the automatic stabilizers. The main discretionary spending increases in the budget were for defense (due to Sputnik) and agriculture (because a bumper farm crop had caused price-support outlays to double).

Compared to 1954, the Eisenhower administration performed less well as a Keynesian manager of aggregate demand in 1958. Treasury Secretary Robert Anderson defeated CEA chairman Saulnier in a battle for the president's ear. Saulnier argued that a consumption-boosting tax cut was vital to stimulate the economy, but Anderson insisted that its enlargement of the deficit would only aggravate inflation. Although the economy did pick up in mid-1958, sluggish recovery did nothing to lessen popular disenchantment with Eisenhower's handling of the recession. The Republicans paid a heavy price for his passivity. As Richard Nixon observed, "The power of the 'pocketbook' issue was shown more clearly perhaps in 1958 than in any off-year election in history." A landslide victory gave Democrats their largest majorities in Congress since the 1930s and enabled them to claim a mandate for their expansionary budget agenda.

Eisenhower found himself embroiled in his most difficult budgetary struggle with Congress during his last two years in office. Arguably he won the battle but lost the war. In 1959 congressional Democrats proposed a huge increase in domestic program spending for the FY 1960 budget in order to strengthen recovery. Though Saulnier urged him to counter by proposing a tax cut instead, Eisenhower agreed with Anderson that it was vital to balance the budget in the wake of the FY 1959 deficit. Yet another deficit, they feared, would open the floodgates to inflation and undermine foreign confidence in the dollar. The president went on the attack to alert the public about these dangers. Polls showed that his message hit home. As columnist Richard Strout observed, Eisenhower turned the tables on his Democratic critics "with the bogey words 'inflation,' 'spenders' and 'deficits.'" Buttressed by this success and by the support of the Republican–conservative Democrat congressional coalition, the president used his veto power to frustrate virtually every Democratic effort to increase spending above what he proposed. As a result, the FY 1960 budget ended up in balance. Eisenhower planned to follow this with a large surplus in his final FY 1961 budget.

But the economy slipped back into recession in late 1960. In American history since 1945, only one expansionary cycle—that of 1980–1981—has been briefer than the one that began in mid-1958. The economy did not operate at anywhere near its full potential, and unemployment remained at a relatively high level during this recovery period. The rapid shift from a massive deficit in FY 1959 to a balanced budget in FY 1960 was unprecedented in peacetime history and denied the economy adequate stimulus. Economists are generally agreed that Eisenhower's strategy was the greatest fiscal policy mistake by any administration between the end of World War II and the Americanization of the Vietnam War in 1965. Once again the Republican party suffered the political consequences of his budgetary principles. Eisenhower remained deaf to Richard Nixon's pleas that he change course to avoid a preelection recession. As the latter feared, rising unemployment was a key factor in his narrow defeat in the 1960 race for the presidency.

Eisenhower's determination to hold firm against the Democratic "spenders" had rebounded on him. His mishandling of fiscal policy in 1959–1960 helped his opponents to recapture the White House. Economic growth was a major issue in John F. Kennedy's presidential campaign—the chain that linked his vision of what needed to be done at home with what needed to be done abroad. Kennedy had declared in the final television debate with Nixon that it was incumbent on the next president "to get this country moving again, to get our economy moving ahead, to set before the American people its goals, its unfinished business." His victory ensured that the United States would have a new budgetary agenda in the 1960s.

# 4

# The Age of Activism, 1961–1968

IN THE 1960s budgetary policy moved away from the fiscal equilibrium of the Truman-Eisenhower era. The Democratic administrations of John F. Kennedy and Lyndon B. Johnson recorded only a single balanced budget between them. They placed more emphasis on balancing the budget at the hypothetical full-employment level than at the actual level of receipts and outlays. This "new economics" represented the triumph of liberal Keynesian ideas first advanced during World War II: it used the budget to expand the productive capacity of the American economy. The tax cut of 1964 was the cornerstone of this policy. The resultant economic growth produced a harvest of extra revenue that funded a major expansion of domestic programs in the mid-1960s. Meanwhile, the Americanization of the Vietnam War made additional demands on the nation's purse. The huge increase in defense and domestic outlays fueled inflationary pressures that rose in the buoyant economy during the second half of the decade. The economy was now in need of restraint rather than expansion, but the new economics proved less adept at this task. By the end of the 1960s the United States was in the grip of an inflationary spiral that budgetary policy had helped to create.

## THE NEW ECONOMICS

Kennedy took office with ambitious plans to restore America's military ascendancy, to meet the challenge of communism in the Third World, to win the space race with the Soviets, and to enact his New Frontier program of domestic reform. All this would cost a great deal of money. Yet the Democratic platform in the 1960 election contained an explicit commitment to balance the budget except in times of national emergency or recession. This bore testimony to the political success of the antideficit campaign waged by President Eisenhower during his final two years in office. Kennedy's election statements avowed that economic growth would provide the extra revenue to fund budgetary expansion without recourse to deficits. Equally important, it would obviate the need for tax increases. Economic growth seemingly offered a recipe for a new political consensus. What the Democrats promised was to enlarge the economic pie rather than reslice it into more equal portions. This enabled them to fulfill their historic mission to improve the material conditions of low-income Americans without having to redistribute wealth from upper-income groups and the expanding middle class. Kennedy's elixir for generating growth was interest rate reduction to provide cheap credit, but the need to stem the gold drain had undermined this monetary strategy even before he took office.

Having accumulated most of the world's supply of gold during World War II, the United States acted as world banker after the war. The Bretton Woods agreement of 1944, signed by forty-four nations, created a gold exchange standard as the mechanism for a new global monetary order. It established the dollar as the international reserve currency, convertible into gold at $35 an ounce, and committed the U.S. to redeem foreign-held dollars in gold whenever required. After 1945 America ran a virtually continuous international balance-of-payments deficit. A huge outflow of dollars in the form of aid, military expenditures, investments, and import payments provided the world trade system with much-needed liquidity. The U.S. gold reserve position did not come under threat while nations engaged in postwar reconstruction found it useful to build up dollar reserves. By 1960, however, Western Europe and Japan had achieved recovery and had begun to convert surplus dollars into gold. This trend accelerated as a result of Kennedy's pronouncements about easy money, which international opinion regarded as the first step toward a dollar devaluation. In reality America's currency was overvalued in light of its trading competitors' resurgence. But Kennedy regarded a strong dollar as crucial to America's world power. To allay foreign concern, he promised on election eve not to devalue and modified his position on interest rates. In doing so, he closed off the monetary route to economic growth.

Kennedy therefore took office with no clear idea as to how to get the economy growing again. By contrast, his Council of Economic Advisers (CEA) had no doubts about what needed to be done. The election of a Democratic president ensured that this body would be staffed by Keynesian economists drawn from the nation's top universities. It was their belief that the economy was suffering from chronic slack which could only be redressed through an infusion of fiscal adrenaline. This represented a shift beyond the countercyclical application of Keynesianism to a position that the new CEA chairman, Walter H. Heller of the University of Minnesota, described as "Keynes cum growth." Instead of smoothing the business cycle, the objective of this "new economics" was the continuous expansion of productive output (GNP) and the closing of the gap between actual output and the economy's expanding potential. Keynesians estimated a performance gap of almost $50 billion between potential GNP at full-employment level and actual output in the economy that Kennedy had inherited from Eisenhower. In their view, fiscal policy had to be used to close this gap and keep it shut as growth advanced.

The new economics was more interested in balancing the economy than balancing the budget. The Kennedy CEA wanted the budget to be calculated in terms of the hypothetical level of receipts if the economy were operating at full employment, defined as a jobless rate of 4 percent or less, rather than the actual level of receipts. This approach factored growth into budget policy. Full employment was a moving target since the labor force was continuously expanding in numbers and productivity improvements were constantly replacing jobs with technology. Accordingly, the "full-employment budget" provided a more accurate measure of whether fiscal policy was expansionary or not. A full-employment deficit (that is, a deficit even if the economy were at full employment) indicated a stimulative budget, a full-employment surplus the reverse. Measured on this basis, Eisenhower's actual deficit of $3.3 billion in FY 1961 amounted to a restrictive hypothetical surplus of $10 billion.

Taking their cue from Keynes, the new economists regarded the expansion of consumption as the motor of economic growth. "What we seek," avowed Heller, "is an increase in the total demand in the economy, a removal, as it were, of the fiscal drag on spending in the country." From the CEA's perspective, the main cause of fiscal drag was the built-in flexibility of the tax system. Though a good cushion against recession, the automatic stabilizers pushed up tax receipts as soon as the economy showed signs of recovery, thereby cutting into the growth of private income in advance of the achievement of full employment. The consequent retardation of economic expansion was the main cause of the performance gap between potential and real GNP. A fiscal dividend was needed to sustain the growth in aggregate demand, which meant either reducing taxes or increasing expenditures. Heller and his CEA colleagues favored the first option for both economic and political reasons. In their view, a tax cut was much more effective as a quick-acting stimulant than increased spending, whose benefits could be dissipated by pork-barrel projects, waste, and bottlenecks. Tax reduction was also much more likely to win approval from Congress. And it was less likely to set off a new outflow of gold, since international financiers would be more tolerant of a tax-induced deficit than one resulting from expenditure growth.

The triumph of the new economics over traditional budget balancing was by no means assured. At first the CEA had little support within the corridors of power. In early 1961 it urged Kennedy to propose a $9.5 billion tax cut as a means of generating a further $20 billion of GNP, courtesy of the magic effect of the Keynesian multiplier. The complementary boost given to business investment by rising consumer demand was expected to make up a further $10 billion. But the presidential ear was unreceptive. Knowing that many corporate leaders distrusted him as a big-spending liberal, Kennedy worried that a deficit budget policy would undermine business confidence and thereby damage the economy. The narrowness of his presidential election victory had weakened his leverage over Congress, thus his spending program would be vulnerable to conservative Democratic and Republican demands for budget-balancing retrenchment to pay for a tax cut. Finally, Kennedy was uncomfortably aware that tax reduction flew in the face of his Inaugural Address call for national sacrifice to meet the domestic and international challenges of the 1960s.

The CEA nevertheless won a small victory for expansionary spending. Signs that the economy was moving out of the brief recession inherited from Eisenhower encouraged Kennedy to propose a balanced budget for FY 1962. He soon found it necessary to request large supplemental defense appropriations as a result of escalating cold war tensions. Kennedy had originally intended to fund the increase in military spending through increased taxation, but he was persuaded by the CEA that this would harm the economy. As a result, the FY 1962 budget was allowed to run up a $7.2 billion deficit, which helped to reduce the performance gap in the economy to $30 billion.

This was not enough to convert the president to the new economics. More important was the change in his attitude toward the business community. Kennedy had made every effort to break down the well-publicized suspicions of corporate leaders that he was antibusiness. He had appointed top businessmen to his cabinet and promoted a tax-relief bill in 1962 to boost business investment in plants and capital goods. He also sought to establish his credentials as an inflation-fighter. In early 1962 the administration persuaded the steel unions to accept a modest wage settlement in the expectation that the steel companies would then hold their prices steady. But United States Steel and several other firms abruptly raised prices. Enraged, Kennedy used every weapon at his disposal, including a threat to withhold defense contracts from the offending companies, to whip them back into line. Corporate leaders saw this as proof of his animus against business. U.S. Chamber of Commerce president Richard Wagner warned, "We should remember that dictators in other lands usually come to power through constitutional procedures." Shortly afterward, the stock market suffered its worst decline since 1929, a collapse widely attributed to business fears about Kennedy. These developments transformed the president's outlook. Now convinced that nothing he did would please business, he no longer felt the need to appease it with balanced budgets. And since he could not rely on business confidence to sustain economic growth, he became more receptive to the new economics.

Kennedy's address at Yale University on June 11, 1962, challenged head-on the old fiscal orthodoxies. "The myth persists," he declared, "that federal deficits create inflation and budget surpluses prevent it.... Obviously deficits are sometimes dangerous—and so are surpluses. But honest assessment plainly requires a more sophisticated view than the old and automatic cliché that deficits automatically bring inflation.... What we need is not labels and chichés but more basic discussion of the sophisticated and technical questions involved in keeping a great economic machine moving ahead.... What is at stake in our economic decisions today is not some grand warfare of rival ideologies which will sweep the country with passion but the practical management of a modern economy."

This speech marked Kennedy as the first president who aspired to break fully from balanced budgets. Nevertheless, the transformation of rhetoric into reality was a tortuous process. The president continued to dither about when to propose the large tax cut sought by the CEA. Administration allies on Capitol Hill warned that Congress would probably balk at tax reduction unless there were signs of economic slowdown. The Treasury worried that European bankers would rush to convert their dollar holdings into gold out of concern that the inflationary consequences of cutting taxes when the economy was not in recession would force the United States to devalue the dollar.

What bolstered Kennedy's nerve were signs that his public advocacy of the new economics was winning the hearts and minds of the business community. As indicated by the enthusiastic response to his address to the Economic Club of New York in December 1962, many corporate leaders had finally come to believe that tax reduction would do more than balanced budgets for the economy. Meanwhile, the CEA had succeeded in persuading Treasury Secretary Douglas Dillon that stronger economic growth would work to the dollar's advantage, but it made important concessions to win his support for the tax cut. The tax bill eventually sent to Congress proposed a tax reduction of $13.5 billion, partially offset by the inclusion of Treasury proposals for tax reform that would yield $3.5 billion in extra revenue by closing tax loopholes for business. Tax reduction was also to be phased over three years instead of concentrated into one. These changes also suited the president, since they spared him the embarrassment of projecting a larger deficit in FY 1964 than Eisenhower's record FY 1959 deficit.

Kennedy proposed the tax cut in January 1963 but did not live to see the measure enacted. After prolonged wrangling and compromise, the House of Representatives approved it in September, just two months before Kennedy's assassination. The cause of dispute was tax reform rather than tax reduction. Besieged by an army of tax lobbyists, the Ways and Means Committee did not release the bill until the administration agreed to remove its loophole-closing provisions. As compensation for the resultant loss of revenue, the amount of tax reduction was clawed back to $10 billion. A potentially more difficult battle loomed in the Senate where conservative Democrats and Republicans, who dominated the all-important

Finance Committee, demanded offsetting economies in spending to ensure that tax cuts did not lead to a huge budget deficit. Anxious to avoid conflict at the outset of his administration, Lyndon Johnson made tactical concessions that facilitated speedy enactment of the bill in February 1964. The new president scaled back spending plans for the FY 1965 administrative budget to $98 billion, $4 billion below the ceiling approved by Kennedy. But he kept faith with his predecessor's Keynesian legacy by shifting more of the tax cut into calendar 1964 and compressing it into two years.

The new economics had finally triumphed over the last vestiges of balanced-budget doctrine, namely that federal revenue should exceed outlays when the economy was not in recession. The 1964 tax cut marked the completion of the fiscal revolution begun in the early 1930s. Arthur Okun, who became CEA chairman in 1968, observed that it was "the first major stimulative measure adopted in the post-war era at a time when the economy was neither in, nor threatened imminently by, recession. And unlike U.S. tax reductions in the 1920s, late 1940s, and 1954, the 1964 action was taken in a budgetary situation marked by the twin facts that the federal budget was in deficit and federal expenditures were rising." Nor was it intended to provide relief from high taxes imposed in wartime, as had been the case with the tax measures of the 1920s and 1948. The lack of progressive features was also unusual in view of the measure's Democratic paternity. For the large majority of taxpayers in the $5,000 to $50,000 income range, who accounted for about 60 percent of all taxable returns and 80 percent of tax liabilities under existing law, the cuts were roughly similar. Arguments for economic justice and wealth redistribution were absent from Kennedy's tax-cutting rhetoric. Instead his goal had been to move tax policy away from the revenue-raising concerns of the Roosevelt, Truman, and Eisenhower administrations and to make it an integral element of pro-growth fiscal policy.

The economy's performance after the tax cut bore out the CEA's most optimistic predictions. GNP grew in real terms by 5.5 percent in calendar 1964 and by 6.3 percent the following year. Unemployment fell to 4.1 percent in 1965, effectively the full-employment rate. The deficit actually shrank from $5.9 billion (.9 percent of GNP) in FY 1964 to $1.5 billion (.2 percent of GNP) in FY 1965. Meanwhile, inflation remained reassuringly low. Even conservative Republicans and right-wing businessmen had to acknowledge that the tax cut had worked wonders. The new economics also won lavish praise from the media. Its crowning glory came in December 1965: the long-dead John Maynard Keynes finally made the front cover of *Time*, which carried an article entitled "We Are All Keynesians Now."

## Defense, Doctrines, and Dollars

After the enactment of the tax cut, the political focus of budgetary policy switched to spending issues. By then the military expansion of the early 1960s had run its course and given way to a new period of defense cost-containment. Both Kennedy and Johnson anticipated that the extra revenues generated by economic growth would go to pay for domestic program expansion. But the Americanization of the Vietnam War in 1965 threw budgetary policy into disarray.

Kennedy had entered office determined to push for higher levels of defense expenditure. A supporter of "flexible response" doctrine, he sought greater balance between America's strategic, conventional, and limited-war capabilities in order to meet the Communist challenge at different force levels. In pursuit of this strategy and in response to cold war crises over Berlin in 1961 and Cuba in 1962, defense spending was increased in FY 1961–1963 by some 10 percent in current dollar terms above Eisenhower's projections. The extra funding went toward strategic force buildup, especially Minuteman missiles and Polaris submarines, and conventional force improvements, notably army expansion from fourteen to sixteen divisions and the enhancement of airlift and sealift capabilities for deployment of limited-war forces. Nevertheless, the budgetary increases were less dramatic than Kennedy's rhetoric suggested. In constant dollar terms annual defense outlays in FY 1961–1963 were on average only 1.4 percent higher than in FY 1958–1960.

The cycle of military expansion had weakened before Kennedy's death. By then "mutual assured destruction" (MAD) doctrine had replaced counterforce doctrine as the core of his administration's nuclear strategy. Counterforce doctrine assumed that in a crisis, nuclear supremacy would enable the U.S. to launch a surgical first strike capable of destroying Russia's nuclear forces. By contrast, MAD contended that even a victorious nuclear war would result in mass death for millions of Americans. The new thinking was promoted by Secretary of Defense Robert S. McNamara, who grew increasingly skeptical that a nuclear war was winnable in light of Soviet measures to expand their missile armory, harden their launch sites, and deploy more nuclear submarines in 1962–1963. In his view these developments proved that a U.S. strategic buildup had little value because it would inevitably be countered by the Russians. Accordingly, McNamara advocated that strategic balance between the superpowers offered the best safeguard against nuclear war. This mutual-deterrence doctrine provided the rationale for defense retrenchment in the mid-1960s.

Further economies were afforded through the introduction

by McNamara (a former president of the Ford Motor Company) of modern management techniques to the Pentagon. In particular, the "planning-programming budget," first used in preparing the FY 1963 defense estimates, provided systematic comparisons of the costs and benefits of alternative programs and systems. It imposed a relatively high degree of centralized control over weapons procurement, thereby depriving the armed services of their traditional autonomy to push for pet projects. The effect was to reduce waste, duplication, and excess. Programs affected by this exercise included the B-70 manned bomber, the nuclear surface fleet, and new fighter aircraft.

Military spending was stabilized in Kennedy's final budget in FY 1964. It was reduced by over $4 billion (7.7 percent) in Johnson's first budget, which was also the last pre–Vietnam War budget. National defense expenditure amounted to $50.6 billion in FY 1965, the lowest level in real terms since the first year of the Korean War. This also represented its smallest share of total budget outlays (42.8 percent) and of GNP (7.5 percent) since FY 1950. In its rationale, strategic-balance doctrine had much in common with Eisenhower's revised New Look. Paradoxically, it made possible defense cutbacks that led to military resentment and public remarks about presidential penny-pinching on national security—the same kinds of criticisms that Kennedy and Johnson had made about Eisenhower's budgets in 1960. Still, the Kennedy-Johnson defense budgets of FY 1964–1965 were different from Eisenhower's in one crucial respect. Where Eisenhower sought retrenchment out of fear of the inflationary effect of big defense spending on the economy, Kennedy and Johnson were intent on redistributing fiscal resources from military to domestic programs. Johnson's budget proposals for FY 1966, unveiled shortly after his landslide reelection victory of

1964, aimed to continue this trend, but the escalation of the Vietnam War upset his calculations.

In mid-1965 Johnson decided to commit the United States to a land war to preserve South Vietnam from a Communist insurgency backed by North Vietnam. This conflict became the ultimate test of America's capacity and will to sustain the doctrine of containment on a global basis. South Vietnam had received American financial and military advisory assistance for nearly a decade. Johnson believed that its defeat would encourage aggression by Soviet surrogates elsewhere in the world. The Communist aim in Vietnam, he told Congress, "is to show that the American commitment is worthless. Once that is done, the gates are down and the road is open to endless conquest and expansion."

How long the lid could have been kept on defense spending had Vietnam not occurred remains a matter of conjecture. Strategic-balance doctrine permitted savings on nuclear arms in the mid-1960s because the preceding defense expansion had endowed the United States with formidable superiority in retaliatory force levels. But Soviet advances, particularly in antiballistic missile (ABM) systems, led to a new cycle of increased spending on strategic forces within a few years. By then the Vietnam War had already made a huge impact on the budget.

The fiscal cost of the war alone in FY 1965–1969 exceeded $80 billion. The first funding specifically earmarked for Vietnam was a $700 million supplemental appropriation to the FY 1965 budget, which Johnson requested in May 1965; but the bulk of this could not be spent in the short time before the fiscal year ended. War outlays rose only to $5.6 billion the following year. The United States had a large standing army and a huge store of military supplies. The cost of shifting part of this existing force, which carried the main burden of fighting in the first year of the war, was relatively low. It was not until FY 1967 that expenditure on Vietnam really skyrocketed, because of the need for extra troops, more weaponry, and additional bombers (plus replacements for planes shot down) as the conflict went on. War costs of $19.4 billion were nearly double what Johnson had estimated in his original budget proposals. In FY 1968, when U.S. force levels exceeded 500,000, outlays on Vietnam rose again to $26.5 billion.

Antiwar sentiment in Congress was weak. The FY 1965 emergency appropriation was approved within three days after Johnson submitted it. This was a notable event, for the president had made it clear that he would regard the vote as an expression of support for his Vietnam policy—even though he did not clarify his intention to expand the land war. To all intents and purposes Johnson used this budgetary enactment as the equivalent of a declaration of war by Congress. In later years he would cite it as proof that he had consulted the legislature over the Americanization of the war. Congress continued to approve war appropriations in spite of the growth of antiwar opinion in the country. Only in the early 1970s did it finally use the power of the purse to restrict presidential war-making in Southeast Asia. During the Johnson years, by contrast, Congress was reluctant to deny money that the commander-in-chief deemed essential for the effectiveness of U.S. forces in the field. An effort to attach a rider to a FY 1967 supplemental appropriation prohibiting the use of the money for the bombing of North Vietnam attracted only eighteen votes in the House of Representatives.

Meanwhile, the war helped to loosen restraints on other forms of military expenditure. The savings yielded by McNamara's budgeting system were whittled away in FY

1967–1968. Congress voted higher defense funds than Johnson requested in order to finance long-stymied projects like ABM deployment, nuclear-powered guided-missile frigates, and the B-70 manned bomber. The administration was in a weak position to counter this expansion in view of its own fiscal excess in Vietnam and its need to sustain congressional support for ever-increasing war appropriations. Moreover, the war strengthened the influence, at least in the short term, of what Eisenhower had called the military-industrial complex, the interrelationship of public bureaucracies and private corporations with a common interest in bigger defense budgets. With defense needs preeminent on the budgetary agenda, members of Congress were more receptive to warnings from the armed services that long-term projects unrelated to Vietnam should not be neglected, and to the enticements of defense firms that military contracts meant more jobs for their states and districts.

In FY 1968 total spending on national defense was some $31 billion higher in current dollar terms than in FY 1965, a real increase of 35 percent. In constant dollar terms, this was the highest level since the final year of the Korean War. During Korea, however, defense's share of the budget increased from 32 percent in FY 1950 to 69 percent in FY 1953. During Vietnam, it rose only from 43 percent in FY 1965 to 46 percent in FY 1968. This was because Lyndon Johnson was the only president in American history to launch a major program of reform while the country was fighting a war. The United States therefore found itself in a unique fiscal position in the second half of the 1960s when both the defense and domestic budgets underwent significant expansion.

## THE GREAT SOCIETY

Johnson's Great Society programs constituted the greatest outburst of reform since the 1930s. Skillfully exploiting national remorse following Kennedy's assassination, the new president persuaded Congress to enact a number of bills it had previously blocked. His landslide reelection in 1964 provided a mandate for further reform and massive Democratic majorities in both houses of the legislature. As a result, the power of the conservative coalition to obstruct liberal legislation was finally broken in the Eighty-ninth Congress of 1965–1966.

Like the New Deal, the Great Society encompassed programs that were nonbudgetary in nature (such as civil rights, consumer protection, and immigration law reform), but most of its enactments had fiscal consequences. Unlike the New Deal, it was not a response to economic depression but sought to make the promise of American life a reality for all citizens regardless of race or class. In many respects the social objectives of the Great Society were interlinked with the new economics. This was particularly true of its antipoverty program, which sought to equip the poor to take advantage of job opportunities generated by an expanding economy. At a time when it was unaware of how much Vietnam would eventually cost, the CEA reassured Johnson that economic expansion would more than pay for increased domestic outlays without necessitating a budget deficit. This prediction proved accurate. Leaving aside Social Security (a self-financed program), the increase in domestic program expenditure accounted for just under three-fifths of the expansion in tax revenues that would have occurred between FY 1965 and FY 1969 had the economy continued on its noninflationary, high-employment growth track.

Perhaps inevitably, the Great Society's achievements fell far short of its ambitious agenda, so it failed to lay the foundations for a new political consensus. Its legacy remains a source of controversy to the present day. Contemporary conservatives see it as the progenitor of welfare dependency, bureaucratic overregulation, wasteful public spending, and spiraling deficits. Ronald Reagan's efforts to reduce big government were mainly directed at the Great Society's creations rather than the New Deal's.

Judged on budgetary terms, however, the Great Society does not merit the calumny of its conservative critics. Many of Johnson's initiatives bore modest costs at the time. Not until the 1970s, after he had left office, was more generous funding provided for his programs. Even though Johnson identified the eradication of poverty as the Great Society's chief aim, its social program outlays benefited the nonpoor far more than the poor. And the war in Vietnam took precedence over the Great Society in Johnson's later budgets.

Federal spending on human resource programs rose from 5.4 percent of GNP in FY 1965 to 7 percent in FY 1968. Much of this increase went to pay for the Great Society's expansion of the Social Security program and its introduction of Medicare to provide health-care insurance for the aged. By FY 1969 these two programs accounted for about half of total human resource outlays, but Social Security taxes had also been increased to ensure the continuing solvency of the system. The Great Society spent significantly less on welfare improvements funded from administrative budget taxes, such as the liberalization of Aid to Families with Dependent Children, the introduction of Medicaid health-care assistance for the poor, aid-to-education for impoverished school districts, and the much ballyhooed War on Poverty. The Office of Economic Opportunity received an annual budget averaging

$1.7 billion to fund War on Poverty initiatives like community action, the Head Start preschool program, and job-training schemes. This was equivalent to between $50 and $65 a year per poor person, and much of this inadequate money went to program administration.

In spite of the fulminations of Reagan-era conservatives, the Great Society's antipoverty measures were not a fiscal black hole for the tax dollars of hard-working Americans. Between FY 1965 and FY 1980, federal expenditures on programs targeted at poor people and requiring proof of need to qualify for benefits rose from 4 percent to 9 percent of total budget outlays. In the same period, federal benefits not targeted at poor people and not involving a test of need (such as Social Security, Medicare, and veterans' benefits) rose from 24 percent of the budget to 40 percent. In FY 1980 only about one-fifth of total federal benefit payments went to help citizens living in poverty rise out of it. The rest went to people who were not poor. The Great Society did not redistribute wealth from the affluent to the impoverished. Instead, as economist Herbert Stein noted, it "ended up as a gigantic program for transferring income to middle-income people—mainly old—from middle-income people—mainly of working age."

Johnson's innovations turned out to be much more expensive in the long term than envisaged in the 1960s. In FY 1965 social welfare programs (not including veterans' benefits) cost $31 billion, 26 percent of the budget and 4.5 percent of GNP. Four years later the parallel statistics were $59 billion, 32 percent, and 6.7 percent. By FY 1980 the costs had risen to $280 billion, 48 percent of the budget, and 11 percent of GNP. In constant-dollar terms, this represented an increase of over 300 percent since FY 1965, five times the real growth in GNP. Johnson and his advisers had expected some expansion, but nothing on this scale. They failed to anticipate that increased life expectancy would affect social insurance outlays; that the availability of cheap or free health care would increase demand for medical services and consequently inflate the costs charged for medical care; and that the Great Society's insistence that welfare was a right for the poor would encourage more widespread application for public assistance. Nor could anyone have foreseen the substantial increases in Social Security benefits enacted in the unusual political and economic circumstances of the early 1970s, when high inflation and electoral competition between a Republican president and a Democratic Congress combined to produce program expansion.

The Great Society also expanded physical resource programs, but the short-term budgetary effects were slight. Federal spending in this area increased by one-third in real terms during the 1960s. As in the New Deal era, the bulk of outlays went to agriculture, resource development, and transportation. This was in spite of the Johnson administration's efforts to diversify federal spending in favor of new programs in environmental protection, conservation, housing, urban renewal, and regional development. In this respect, expenditure trends did not correspond with the legislative output of the Great Society. New laws to regulate water and air quality put the federal government in the forefront of pollution control. Other initiatives sought to provide development assistance to depressed areas like Appalachia. The Department of Housing and Urban Development was created to coordinate federal efforts to improve housing, employment opportunities, and the social fabric in inner-city areas.

The large gaps between legislative objectives and budgetary appropriations for these new programs occurred mainly because the Vietnam War and social welfare initiatives had fiscal priority. In the case of water pollution control, for example, the Johnson administration consistently requested appropriations of less than half the funds that Congress had authorized for this purpose. Constraints on funding for physical resources also meant that new measures had to compete for money with well-established programs. Many members of Congress were unwilling to vote large appropriations for those Great Society programs that did not provide the pork-barrel benefits of traditional public works. Partly for this reason, funding for the new urban policies, whose concerns extended far beyond construction projects, consistently fell short of administration targets.

Transportation remained the best funded of the physical resource programs, accounting for nearly two-fifths of total spending in this area. The increase in its outlays during the 1960s was greater than the combined increase in spending for all housing, urban, and regional development programs. The ways the money was spent were little changed. Great Society efforts to boost mass transit were poorly funded. By contrast, the interstate highway system continued to be generously financed, even though, by the mid 1960s, costs had nearly doubled over initial projections. Far from seeking cost control, Congress increased the program's mileage and stretched out its completion date. Highway and gasoline taxes were raised to pay for this.

As with social welfare, the Great Society's physical resource initiatives laid the foundations for greater future spending. In some respects this was inevitable in view of the comparatively low funding levels at which many of these programs began. The new political agenda of the 1970s, marked by increasing concern about energy shortages, environmental pollution, and the deindustrialization of urban areas, also worked in their favor. Finally, the American withdrawal from Vietnam weakened political restraints on domestic spending.

In his memoirs Johnson claimed, "I was never convinced that Congress would have voted appreciably more funds for domestic programs if there had been no struggle in Southeast Asia. If we had succeeded in stilling the guns in Vietnam, as we tried so desperately to do, I believe that many Congressmen would have demanded tax reductions rather than providing increased funds for the beleaguered cities." It was his belief that Republican gains in the midterm congressional elections of 1966 killed off the prospects for major expansion of the Great Society during his final two years in office. Although Democrats retained a majority, the power of the conservative coalition in Congress was restored. The elections also testified to the changing mood of the electorate that had handed the Democrats a landslide victory two years earlier. A wave of ghetto riots in 1965 had generated a backlash against the social activism of the federal government. Many white voters now felt that the Great Society was more intent on aiding racial minorities and welfare recipients than preserving law and order.

Notwithstanding the changed political circumstances of 1967–1968, Johnson's claim that Vietnam had not constrained the domestic budget was disingenuous. The war gave conservative congressmen an excuse to limit funding for social programs to which they objected on ideological grounds. It consumed the president's energies, which might otherwise have been employed in promoting the advancement of domestic spending measures. Finally, Vietnam's rising costs led to enlarged deficits that constrained the administration's domestic agenda and inhibited it from giving serious consideration to costly new reforms. Nothing demonstrated this better than Johnson's response to the 1968 report of the

National Advisory Commission on Civil Disorders, which he had set up to investigate the causes of another outbreak of ghetto riots in 1967. The commission blamed the riots on the racial discrimination and socioeconomic deprivation that blighted the lives of black ghetto dwellers. Among the solutions it advocated to remedy these conditions were massive increases of federal funds for the welfare, training, job-creation, educational, and urban aid programs of the Great Society. According to Bureau of the Budget estimates, the costs would run at about $30 billion in addition to what was already being spent to combat poverty. Seeing this as utterly unrealistic, Johnson ignored the commission's recommendations, much to the disappointment of some of his aides and of liberal Democrats like Senator Robert Kennedy of New York.

The report on ghetto disorders appeared at the very moment the president was locked in dispute with Congress over antiinflation measures. Many conservative congressmen would not agree to his proposal for a tax increase unless it was accompanied by cutbacks in domestic spending. "I will never understand," he later complained, "how the commission expected me to get this same Congress to turn 180 degrees overnight and appropriate an additional $30 billion for the same programs that it was demanding I cut by $6 billion. This would have required a miracle." This assessment, accurate insofar as it went, left much unsaid. Johnson would have had more room to maneuver for extra social expenditures had the United States not been involved in Vietnam, because the inflation issue would have been less pressing. Admittedly, it is inconceivable that $30 billion—or anything near—would have been appropriated, but it is equally unlikely that the president would not have worked hard to build support for an increased fiscal commitment to address the ghetto crisis.

## GUNS, BUTTER, AND INFLATION

"I believe," Johnson told Congress in 1966, "that we can continue the Great Society while we fight in Vietnam." This guns-*and*-butter policy was unprecedented in the budgetary history of the United States. Many of Johnson's critics—at the time and later—insisted that the United States could not afford to pursue both these goals at the same time. In fact it could afford to do so, and did—but at a cost. The increase in federal spending to pay for the Great Society and Vietnam occurred at a time when the economy was operating at or near its full potential, thanks to the 1964 tax cut and Federal Reserve credit relaxation. The effect was to fuel inflation. From late 1965 onward the primary concern of fiscal policy was to keep the economy from overheating. It was less successful in this task than it had been in promoting economic growth in the early and mid-1960s.

In contrast to Roosevelt in World War II and Truman in Korea, Johnson did not intend to raise taxes to pay for Vietnam. This was a decision largely based on political calculation. Confident of rapid victory, the president did not wish to undermine popular support for the war by asking for a tax increase. He was also well aware that conservatives in Congress would demand domestic retrenchment if he tried to raise taxes. Johnson was determined not to sacrifice "the woman I really loved" (the Great Society) for "that bitch of a war." Finally, a tax increase would slow economic growth, the fundamental prop of the mid-1960s domestic consensus. With good cause, Johnson feared that middle-income Americans would be less willing to support programs that benefited low-income Americans if their own standard of living ceased to rise.

The CEA's initial assessment also reassured Johnson. In July 1965 new chairman Gardner Ackley informed him, "We are certainly not saying that a Vietnam crisis is just what the doctor ordered for the American economy in the next 12 months. But on a coldly objective analysis, the overall effects are most likely to be favorable to our economy." The CEA was concerned that the effects of the 1964 tax cut were wearing off. It wanted a new round of tax cuts of some $6 billion—or an equivalent increase in spending—to keep the economy heading toward full employment. This was more or less what Vietnam would cost in its first year.

By the end of 1965, however, the CEA expressed concern that the economy was in danger of "too much steam." It is an iron law of economics that when aggregate demand for goods and services rises faster than production can be expanded, the result is to bid up prices. Put another way, the excess of demand over supply produces inflation. This was now happening in the American economy. Business investment and consumer spending substantially exceeded government estimates. Federal spending was also on the rise. In FY 1996 the ratio of budget outlays to GNP went up for the first time in four years. U.S. involvement in Vietnam also exacerbated the strains on the economy, even though initial outlays for the war were relatively small. In early 1966 many firms began to stockpile raw materials and intermediate goods for the defense industries in anticipation of shortages as military demand rose.

The new economics now faced a new challenge. This doctrine had envisaged the active, positive, and continuous use of the budget to maintain demand at levels that sustained economic growth without inflation. Fiscal policy could try to cool the overheated economy in one of two ways. Federal spending could be reduced—but this would impair the

Johnson administration's commitment to build the Great Society at home and fight communism in Vietnam. The only alternative, therefore, was to increase taxes to siphon off spending power from the private economy. This would sustain public demand at the expense of private demand. Significantly, the CEA did not justify the tax increase as necessary to pay for government programs. True to their creed, the new economists focused their concern on the fine-tuning of demand rather than the elimination of the deficit. Admittedly, the imbalance between outlays and receipts was only $3.7 billion (.5 percent of GNP) in FY 1966, and was hardly a critical inflationary force. But the CEA did not retreat into balanced-budget rhetoric as the deficit widened to $8.6 billion (1.1 percent of GNP) in FY 1967 and to a postwar record of $25.2 billion (3 percent of GNP) in FY 1968.

With the FY 1967 budget in its final planning stage, Ackley informed Johnson in December 1965, "If the budget is $115 billion, there is little question in my mind that a significant tax increase will be needed to prevent an intolerable degree of inflationary pressure. With a budget of $110 billion, the question is more difficult. My tentative view now is that a tax increase would probably still be necessary." The president refused to heed this advice. He feared that Congress would not enact a general tax increase but would seize the admission of need for a tighter budget as an excuse to reduce Great Society outlays.

The FY 1967 budget proposals sent to Congress in January 1966 estimated expenditures of $113 billion, including $10.3 billion for the Vietnam War. As the historian Allen Matusow suggests, this represented "a combination of wish projection and deceit" on Johnson's part. Congress was informed that the Vietnam estimate was based on the assumption that the war would end within the fiscal year, though no one involved in Vietnam decision-making truly expected this. The CEA was also misled on this score. In fact, war outlays were nearly double what was projected. The likely extent of the overspending soon became evident. Acting on the CEA's advice, Johnson submitted a supplementary "little budget" as an antiinflation measure in September 1966. Quickly enacted by Congress, this suspended corporate investment tax credits and made some cutbacks in nondefense programs, but it was not enough to curb inflation.

To the CEA Keynesians, the failure to raise personal and corporate income taxes in FY 1967 opened the floodgates to inflation. In Arthur Okun's words, they "watched with pain and frustration as fiscal policy veered off course." The new economics rested on the belief that government could redress the weaknesses inherent in the private economy. Yet the budget itself was now the engine of inflation. Critics of the new economics on both the right and the left later insisted that inflation would have posed an equally serious threat as the economy approached full employment, even if the United States had not been involved in Vietnam. Such judgments are impossible to prove—or disprove. Whatever might have happened in different circumstances, the historical reality is that the new economics foundered on the rocks of politics.

There is good reason to believe that the United States could have had guns, butter, and low inflation if its political leaders had been willing to make a timely increase in taxes. It remains a matter of speculation whether, at a time when the war was relatively popular, Johnson could have persuaded the liberal-inclined Eighty-ninth Congress to raise taxes without endangering the Great Society. But he declined to take the risk. When the president finally bit the bullet, he faced a much more difficult struggle to get the more conservative Ninetieth Congress to do his bidding at a time when public disenchantment with Vietnam was growing.

For a time, monetary policy succeeded in restraining inflation. The Federal Reserve had engineered a credit crunch in mid-1966, but its effects were so severe that the economy nearly tipped into recession in early 1967. To prevent this the monetary authorities relaxed the brakes and fiscal policy followed suit with the restoration of the investment tax credit. But renewed expansion brought with it the threat of accelerating inflation. Signs that the FY 1968 deficit would again be much higher than anticipated also made the president nervous. In these circumstances, Johnson sent a special message to Congress in August 1967 proposing a temporary surcharge of 10 percent on personal and corporate income taxes. This tax on a tax would not raise rates by 10 percent but required individuals and corporations to pay an extra ten cents on every tax dollar. The House Ways and Means Committee, under Democratic chairman Wilbur Mills of Arkansas, voted to lay aside the tax bill until agreement was reached with the administration to reduce domestic outlays.

Johnson thought he could force Mills to back down by taking an unyielding stand against spending cuts, but it was he who gave ground. Britain's devaluation of its inflation-weakened pound in November 1967 aroused fears in world money markets that the United States would follow suit to rescue its own currency. The crisis of confidence in the dollar touched off a new outflow of gold. Johnson now believed that passage of the tax surcharge was essential to reassure foreign bankers that the United States had the will and the ability to keep inflation under control. Though he agreed to accept $4 billion in spending cuts as the price for this, it was not enough to satisfy Mills. There followed months of wrangling over the amount of retrenchment that should accompany the tax increase.

Next to Vietnam, Johnson regarded the tax surcharge as the most important question facing the country in 1968. Early in the year he decided not to seek renomination as president because of the domestic divisions sown by the war. His announcement of this intention in a televised address to the American people on March 31 also contained a forthright warning about the urgency of the tax increase. Johnson hoped that his decision to step down from office would depoliticize the issue and facilitate an agreement with Congress. In reality he remained in a weak bargaining position because of his personal unpopularity over Vietnam and the fact that public opinion opposed the tax increase. Eventually Johnson made a complete surrender in June 1968 by accepting a $6 billion domestic spending reduction in order to win passage of the tax surcharge.

The results of this change in fiscal policy were mixed. It put the budget in the black. The Revenue and Expenditure Control Act was enacted too late to prevent the record FY 1968 deficit, but it helped generate a surplus of $3.2 billion in FY 1969. The budget has not been balanced since. Yet the new economists, who had long urged a restraining tax increase, did not rejoice at this success. In their eyes the movement from a large deficit in FY 1968 to a full-employment surplus of $11.7 billion in FY 1969 was fiscal overkill. The CEA predicted that the effect would flatten the economy into recession, but this did not happen. In fact the tax increase failed to achieve its primary purpose of restraining inflation, which continued to rise. It did little to curtail private spending, partly because its temporary nature did not affect consumers' long-term income expectations, but mainly because of the availability of cheap credit. Sharing CEA fears about a downswing, the Federal Reserve countered the restrictive fiscal policy with an easy-money policy that kept private demand for goods and services buoyant in 1968.

The 1960s ended with the new economics under a cloud, but its balance sheet contained important successes. Fiscal policy had contributed substantially to the elimination of the performance gap in the American economy. Economic growth had proved far more effective in reducing poverty than had government programs targeted at the poor. The fiscal dividend generated by economic growth also allowed for the adjustment of spending priorities within the budget to provide funding for new domestic programs. But the new economics had failed to keep the economy growing without an attendant rise in inflation.

An inflation rate of 3 to 4 percent, as existed in 1967–1968, does not look bad from the perspective of the 1970s. Some new economists, like Kennedy CEA member James Tobin of Yale University, believed this price was worth paying for full employment, but many others were less sanguine. In the late 1960s inflation halted the long postwar rise in the average after-tax earnings of the American industrial worker, reduced the value of business after-tax profits, and brought the worst international crisis of confidence in the dollar since 1931. The overheated economy was also more vulnerable to the effects of supply-side shocks, as would become evident in the early 1970s. It was small wonder, therefore, that Keynesian confidence in the ability of budgetary policy to maintain full employment and expand prosperity, which had shaped liberal economic thought since World War II, would never be as strong again.

# 5

# The Age of Uncertainty, 1969–1980

THE 1970S STAND OUT as an age of uncertainty in the budgetary history of modern America. Fiscal policy was thrown into confusion by the stagflation-prone economy. Keynesian remedies did not work when faced with the unprecedented combination of high inflation, high unemployment, and low growth that afflicted the United States during this period. By the end of the decade, deficits had come to be seen as a cause of rather than a cure for these ills. There was also uncertainty over budgetary priorities. Economic growth had paid for guns and butter in the 1960s, but economic stagnation resulted in the United States having to face difficult choices between domestic and military spending in the 1970s. Meanwhile, inflation weakened the nexus between the expenditure and revenue sides of the budget by generating political pressure for tax reduction at a time when federal outlays were growing. The political tumult of the 1970s also left its mark on the budget. The growing divide between the political parties, the Watergate-era struggle between the presidency and Congress, and the post-Vietnam debate over America's role in world affairs all made it difficult to achieve a consistent approach to spending and taxation.

## The Political Economy of Stagflation

The 1970s proved the most miserable period for the United States economy since the Great Depression of the 1930s. The consumer price index (CPI) rose by 9.3 percent a year on average from 1973 through 1980. Meanwhile, unemployment averaged 5.5 percent in the first half of the 1970s and increased to 7 percent in the second half. Stagflation brought to an end the perpetual increase in living standards that had marked the postwar era. Real median family income, which had nearly doubled between 1947 and 1973, declined by 6 percent between 1973 and 1980. The average worker's spending power was lower in 1980 than it had been in 1970. Small wonder that economic optimism evaporated in these circumstances. One poll taken in 1979 found that two-thirds of respondents agreed that "Americans should get used to the fact that our wealth is limited and most of us are not likely to become better off than we are now."

The economic woes of the 1970s had many roots. The Vietnam War had weakened the economy just as new problems began to appear. America operated in a changed international economy from the late 1960s onward. The pendulum of relative economic power, which World War II had swung toward the United States, now tilted back toward Western Europe and Japan. President Nixon's temporary suspension of gold convertibility in 1971 and his final termination of this currency valuation mechanism in 1973 signified that the dollar was no longer the linchpin of the world monetary order. Increased competition from other nations, not only in the export market but also at home, produced the first U.S. trade deficits of the twentieth century. America's growing dependence on foreign oil, which met a third of its petroleum needs by 1974 as compared with only a fifth in 1960, also made it vulnerable to huge price increases by oil-exporting countries. Inflationary pressures created a vicious circle as trade unions sought cost-of-living wage increases for their members and business passed on these costs to consumers in the form of higher prices. Meanwhile, many American banks and corporations found more to gain from investing overseas than at home: labor costs were cheaper abroad, and tax policy allowed foreign expenses to offset domestic profits. Domestic disinvestment eroded the productivity of America's traditional industries, leading to a wave of plant closures in the Northeast and Midwest during the late 1970s and early 1980s.

The new economics had not succeeded in its aim of fine-tuning the economy to achieve a painless trade-off between full employment and low inflation in the high-growth 1960s. Fiscal policy faced a much more difficult task of economic management in the era of stagflation. Never before had the U.S. economy suffered from such high rates of inflation and unemployment simultaneously. Since these were diametrically opposite problems, measures meant to remedy one tended to aggravate the other. As a result, economic policymakers displayed uncertainty and inconsistency about which needed curing first, inflation or unemployment. Each of the three administrations of the 1970s ended up making something of a U-turn on fiscal policy. In these circumstances economic issues played a more significant role in the political agenda of the 1970s than was the case in the 1960s, when Vietnam, race, law and order, and social issues dominated. Pocketbook concerns did much to decide the outcome of the presidential elections of the 1970s.

Richard Nixon, the victor in the Vietnam-affected presidential election of 1968, inherited an economy that was still relatively in good shape, with full employment and inflation, though high, hardly out of control. As a Republican and a former vice-president in the Eisenhower administration, Nixon could have been expected to make a vigorous assault against inflation, but this pragmatic conservative adopted a middle-way approach to economic policy. Experience had taught him the political dangers of promoting price stability at the expense of jobs. Nixon had blamed his narrow defeat in the 1960 presidential race on the preelection recession brought about by Eisenhower's fiscal restraint. He was determined never again to be the sacrificial lamb on the altar of economic principle. Nixon no longer shared the traditional conservative devotion to balanced budgets as the first line of attack against inflation. He aimed to stabilize prices gradually through a policy of moderate restraint that would not drive unemployment up to unacceptable levels.

Whereas the new economics had relied chiefly on fiscal policy to manage the economy, Nixon and his CEA intended to use monetary policy as well. By the late 1960s Keynesianism was facing a serious challenge to its intellectual ascendancy. Monetarist economists, led by Milton Friedman of the University of Chicago, now contended that the money supply was the major determinant of demand. In their view, deficit budgets did nothing to boost long-term economic growth because public borrowing only served to "crowd out" from the money markets an equivalent amount of private borrowing. In other words, fiscal stimulation was counterbalanced by the contraction of private credit. Monetarists also regarded deficits as an impediment to the orderly management of monetary policy because of the Federal Reserve's obligation to assist government borrowing through its open-market operations. In their view the expansion of the money supply at a faster rate than economic growth was the chief cause of inflation. The new CEA was receptive to this message but not convinced that it was the only true gospel. Reflecting the centrist tone of Nixon's administration, the CEA straddled the middle ground between monetarism and Keynesianism. It labeled itself "Friedmanesque" rather than "Friedmanite" because it thought that "money mattered" in economic management—but not to the exclusion of all else.

Fiscal policy followed the game plan of moderate restraint to the letter. Nixon's first two budgets spent slightly less in real terms than Johnson's final budget. The new administration also extended Johnson's temporary tax surcharge for a twelve-month period, but reduced it from 10 to 5 percent in the final six months. The Federal Reserve, however, charted a different course for monetary policy. Caught up in the progrowth mood of the preceding decade, it had accommodated the expansionary aims of Kennedy-Johnson economic policy in 1962–1965, but had then dithered between seeking to suppress inflation and avoid recession. By 1969 the Fed had decided that inflation had too strong a grip for middle-way measures to work. It now engineered a severe credit crunch that reduced money supply growth almost to zero. This undermined business confidence, with the result that the economy dipped into a mild recession. The downturn of 1969–1970 was historically significant: it ended what was then the longest period of unbroken economic expansion in modern American history; 1960s-style full employment disappeared and has never returned; and, contrary to normal trends, inflation did not fall away as unemployment rose.

Fiscal policy moved from restraint to expansion in response to the recession. Thanks to the automatic stabilizers (declining tax receipts and rising transfer payments), the FY 1971 budget ended up $23 billion in the red. This was the second largest deficit in current dollar terms since World War II, though it represented only a modest 2.2 percent of GNP. Discretionary increases in federal spending helped to produce another bumper deficit of $23.4 billion (2 percent of GNP) in the next budget. Nixon prefaced this by announcing in early 1971, "I am now a Keynesian in economics," a remark greeted by all and sundry as a remarkable conversion. One television journalist commented that it was akin to "a Christian crusader saying, 'All things considered, I think Mohammed was right.'" In reality, of course, Nixon had not undergone a philosophical transformation but was merely seeking to safeguard his reelection prospects by tackling unemployment. More startling was the action he took to ensure that fiscal stimulation of the economy would not aggravate inflationary pressures.

Even as unemployment rose, international developments threatened to exacerbate inflation. With the United States heading toward a merchandise trade deficit in 1971, its first since 1893, the dollar underwent yet another crisis in the world currency markets. The gold convertibility system that had underpinned the international monetary order since 1945 could no longer be sustained. The dollar had to be devalued in order to protect America's gold reserves, but there was a danger that this would fuel inflation at home by making imports more expensive. This led Nixon to gamble on a dramatic new economic policy in August 1971. Its centerpiece was the imposition of the first-ever peacetime controls on prices and wages as a safeguard against the inflationary effects not only of the depreciated dollar but also of expansionary fiscal policy.

Confident that he did not have to worry about inflation for the time being, Nixon set out to create an economic boom to boost his reelection. Every federal department was urged to accelerate its spending plans. The Pentagon, for example, ordered enough trucks to meet its needs for the next several years and stepped up its purchases of many sundry items, including a two-year supply of toilet paper. On this occasion monetary policy was in harmony with fiscal strategy. In response to heavy prodding by the administration, the Federal Reserve permitted a generous expansion of credit. As a result, the economy boomed and inflation and unemployment both fell to acceptable levels in 1972. All this helped Nixon to win a landslide victory in the presidential election over his liberal Democrat opponent, Senator George McGovern of South Dakota.

Nixon justified his expansionary budgets in words that would have sounded more familiar coming from a Democrat. "By spending as if we were at full employment," he declared, "we will help to bring about full employment." A Republican president was now utilizing the economic symbol of 1960s liberalism, but this did not mean that Nixon had become a devotee of the new economics. He regarded the full-employment budget as an instrument of economic stabilization rather than a means of expanding the capacity of the economy. Eliminating the performance gap between actual and potential GNP had no place in his strategy. Nixon always insisted that the budget had to be balanced at the full-employment level in order to safeguard against inflation. This became the goal of his second-term fiscal policy. In January 1973 he announced, "The surest way to avoid inflation or higher taxes or both is for Congress to join me in a concerted effort to control federal spending." Though outlays were not reduced, they remained stable in constant-dollar terms for the remainder of his presidency.

In addition to budgetary restraint, the third phase of "Nixonomics" saw the relaxation and eventual abandonment of wage-price controls. The change of policy seemed to work well at first. As the economy recovered and headed toward full employment, the deficit was substantially reduced to $6.1 billion in FY 1974, the last occasion it has been under $10 billion. Nevertheless, inflation returned with a vengeance. The CPI rose by 8.8 percent in 1973 and by 12.2 percent the following year. International developments played an important part in this. Food prices skyrocketed when crop failures abroad led to increased foreign demand for U.S. farm commodities. Energy costs also rose dramatically as a result of the Arab oil embargo of 1973–1974 and the subsequent decision of the Organization of Petroleum Exporting Countries (OPEC) to quadruple crude oil prices. But supply shocks were not the sole cause of inflation. The Nixon administration was also to blame for pumping up aggregate demand to an unhealthy degree before the 1972 election. Not only did this weaken the wage-price controls when they were in operation, it also added to the stockpile of suppressed inflation that was released during the transition toward decontrol in 1973–1974.

The great inflation contained within it the roots of the great recession. Once again, by tackling one part of the stagflation problem, economic policymakers aggravated the other. The shift toward budgetary restraint proved much too abrupt. A full-employment deficit of $12 billion in calendar 1972 was transformed into a full-employment surplus of $3 billion in calendar 1974. In conjunction with spiraling food prices, the effect was to reduce the growth in aggregate demand to almost zero, even before the oil price shocks made themselves felt. The surplus was almost entirely attributable to the so-called fiscal drag produced by high inflation. Federal tax receipts were buoyant because inflation had pushed wage earners into higher tax brackets and had increased the corporate tax rate by artificially boosting inventory profits and reducing the real value of depreciation allowances. In other words, instead of acting as an automatic stabilizer, the federal tax system had depressed real disposable income just when inflation was eating into purchasing power. The tightening of the monetary screws by the Federal Reserve made matters worse. In late 1974 this combination of factors pushed the economy into the worst recession since the 1930s.

Revelations of his involvement in a cover-up of the Watergate conspiracy led to Nixon's resignation as president just before the recession began. He left office with a disastrous economic record. The failure of the first phase of Nixonomics was mainly attributable to factors beyond his control, namely the difficulties of coordinating fiscal and monetary policy in a political system where the latter is under independent jurisdiction. But the excessive fiscal stimulation that marked the second phase served Nixon's reelection needs better than the economy. True, liberal Democrats who later accused him of using the budget to buy the election were at the time calling for even more expansionary measures, but at least their position was in line with their party's traditions. Nixon's postelection reversion to budget balancing and spending restraints sowed the seeds of recession. Meanwhile, the inflationary bulge caused by supply shocks and wage-price decontrol so consumed economic policymakers' attention that they failed to anticipate the downswing. Nixon's handling of the economic controls ranked among the most serious failures of his flawed presidency. Not only were they misused in 1972, but their termination in the intensely inflationary circumstances of 1974 was a masterpiece of mistiming.

Elevated from vice-president to succeed Nixon, Gerald Ford inherited an economy in worse shape than at any time since the 1930s and a Watergate-weakened presidency incapable of Rooseveltian leadership. His intention was to carry on where his predecessor had left off in economic policy. Seeing inflation as "Public Enemy Number One," Ford was determined to tackle it by balancing the budget, but he soon experienced the policy dilemmas associated with stagflation. The new administration's initial economic program, unveiled in October 1974, called for a temporary tax surcharge of 5 percent and cutbacks in spending programs already authorized for FY 1975. Its focus on inflation at a time when signs of recession were already evident impaired the confidence of the Congress and the public in Ford's economic competence. To make matters worse, the president's accompanying proposal for a Whip Inflation Now program of voluntary citizen involvement in energy and food cost-saving activities was a public relations fiasco. As one observer commented, "Americans were losing their jobs, and Ford was talking about planting radishes in the back yard."

Instead of making progress toward a balanced budget, Ford found himself operating by far the largest deficits since 1945 as a result of the weakened economy. The surge in unemployment compelled him to make a politically embarrassing 180-degree turn to combat the recession. In January 1975 he recommended a one-year across-the-board 10 percent reduction in personal income tax, which would save taxpayers $12 billion, and a $4 billion tax credit to encourage business to initiate new projects. Nevertheless, Ford did not make a similar turnabout on spending, calling instead for a moratorium on new programs (except energy) and a ceiling on existing programs to neutralize the effect of tax reduction on the budget deficit. With inflation still very high (the CPI rose by more than 7 percent in 1975), he attempted a conservative balancing act between competing priorities. Tax reduction was intended to reduce unemployment by giving the private economy a shot in the arm. Conversely, expenditure restraint and deficit control would prevent the economy from overheating in the recovery period, as had happened after the previous recession.

But congressional Democrats were focusing on their party's traditional concern with unemployment, now heading toward a postwar peak of 9.1 percent. Boosted by a landslide victory in the 1974 midterm elections, they enacted a temporary tax cut worth some $23 billion and appropriated $17 billion more for spending programs than recommended by the president. Only Ford's dogged use of the veto to defeat some measures prevented the budget being even larger. This was the first occasion since the fiscal revolution of the 1930s that Congress had seized the economic policy initiative from the president. The last time congressional Democrats had tried to do so was during the late 1950s, but Eisenhower had won that battle. Things were different in 1975 owing to the political fallout from Watergate and the severity of the recession.

The economy improved from mid-1975 onward, but there was no abatement in the political battle over the budget. The Ford administration feared that fiscal drag would harm the recovery when temporary tax reduction expired on January 1, 1976. Yet it was also worried about the deficit, which far surpassed original projections to reach successive postwar highs of $53.2 billion in FY 1975 and $73.7 billion in FY 1976. To resolve this conundrum Ford proposed a permanent tax cut worth $28 billion, contingent on an equivalent reduction in FY 1977 expenditure. But congressional Democrats had no intention of sacrificing spending for the sake of a Republican tax cut and allowing the president to regain control of fiscal policy. They enacted a six-month extension of the income tax cut, worth about $9 billion, without any commitment to expenditure restraint, only to see the measure vetoed by the president. Since neither side wished to be blamed by voters for the loss of tax reduction, there was strong pressure on them to compromise. An alternative measure was duly cobbled together giving the Democrats their tax cut and the White House a vaguely worded guarantee of spending restraint. Predictably, Democratic reluctance to stay within Ford's budget limits led to a resumption of the battle of the vetoes in 1976. On this occasion the president had more success in imposing spending restraints, but FY 1977 appropriations were still well in excess of his target level.

The partisan conflicts of the Ford era indicated that the postwar consensus on political economy had broken down. Since World War II the primary goal of economic management, regardless of which party controlled the White House, had been high employment. Administrations that had focused on inflation, such as Harry Truman's and Dwight Eisenhower's, had done so during periods of economic prosperity. Amidst the most serious economic downturn since the 1930s, the Ford administration had been preoccupied with the inflationary consequences of Keynesianism. The president and top advisers like Treasury Secretary William Simon and CEA chairman Alan Greenspan took the view that big budgets and spiraling deficits achieved only temporary alleviation of unemployment at the cost of aggravating inflationary trends.

Ford's refusal to manipulate the economy to create a preelection boom in 1976 indicated a principled conservative concern to lay the foundations for sustainable long-term growth. In many respects his agenda of tax cuts and spending restraints marked the beginnings of the supply-side revolution that reached its peak under Ronald Reagan. Ford's conservative economics were broadly in tune with those of his party. The Republican platform in the 1976 presidential election labeled inflation as "the number one destroyer of jobs" and the expansion of the money supply to pay for the budget deficit as "the number one cause of inflation." Its prescription for reduced inflation was a strong dose of economy in government and a transference of funds from the public sector to the private sector by means of tax cuts.

By contrast, Democrats remained true to Keynesian ideals. Party leaders in Congress decried Ford's charges that government spending created more problems than it resolved as a throwback to the pre–New Deal past. "We must reject those of timid vision who counsel us to go back," declared Senator Edmund Muskie of Maine. "We cannot go back. We cannot give up. And we will not." The Democratic-controlled congressional Joint Economic Committee condemned Ford's FY 1977 budget plan, even though it projected a deficit of over $50 billion, as "so restrictive that it does not serve as a useful starting point for budgetary deliberations." The party's 1976 platform decreed full employment as the answer to the nation's economic problems, on the grounds that the consequent boost to consumption would lead in turn to business expansion, higher profits, and greater investment. Its fiscal centerpiece was a commitment to enact the Humphrey-Hawkins full-employment bill that required the federal government to reduce unemployment to 3 percent within four years, if necessary by acting itself as the employer of last resort through a public jobs program.

### Losing Faith

Jimmy Carter's defeat of Ford in the 1976 presidential election appeared to reaffirm the political ascendancy of Keynesianism. Economic issues had constituted the most salient policy division between the two candidates. The support of three-quarters of those voters whose primary concern was unemployment had done much to put Carter in the White House. Nevertheless, the transition to more conservative economics was sustained over the next four years. After leaving office Carter entitled his presidential memoirs *Keeping Faith* to symbolize his belief in America's capacity for national redemption after the disasters of Vietnam and Watergate. Ironically, he did not keep faith in the Keynesian doctrines that had shaped his party's fiscal policy and underwritten its political success since the 1930s.

Democratic presidents from Roosevelt through Johnson had promoted a positive image of budget deficits as the instrument to bring about full employment. Carter stood outside the mainstream of his party's fiscal traditions for a number of reasons. In the economic conditions of the 1970s he believed that inflation posed a more serious threat to America's well-being than unemployment. Never having held office at the federal level nor participated in national politics before running for president, Carter had not been exposed to the ideas of the new economics in the 1960s. The formative influence on his fiscal views had been his experience as governor of Georgia. Balanced budgets had continued to be the norm for the states, many of whom were obliged by their constitutions not to operate deficits. No doubt, too, Carter's early career as an engineer predisposed him to value efficiency and scientific management. These principles had no place in Keynesian doctrine, which focused on the macroeconomic effects of the deficit, not the cost-benefit ratio of public spending.

Carter was also the first president from the Deep South since the Civil War. He traced his political lineage not to the New Deal but to early-twentieth-century Southern progressivism, which sought economy and efficiency as well as compassion in government. As such his political views straddled the conventional divides of modern American politics. Carter saw himself as liberal on human issues but conservative in fiscal matters. Dwight Eisenhower, another ideologically ambiguous president, had proffered a similar self-description. Like Ike, Carter aspired to balance the budget by the end of his first term in office, but he never achieved this goal.

During his first six months in office Carter behaved like a traditional Democrat in using fiscal policy to combat unemployment, which was still running high at 7.5 percent. The new administration devised a two-year package of stimulative measures that increased spending by some $15 billion on urban aid, public works, and training. By mid-1977, however, signs that recovery would bring renewed inflation in its wake led to a change of fiscal course. Plans for a tax rebate were scrapped, and the president offended many Democratic congressmen from Western states by his decision to cut spending on water projects in the FY 1978 budget. Carter recalled in his memoirs: "For more than three and a half years, my major economic battle would be against inflation, and I would stay on the side of fiscal prudence, restricted budgets, and lower deficits." In fact, administration policy did not become so clear-cut until somewhat later. Carter presented a modestly expansionary budget for FY 1979 out of concern that the sudden switch to fiscal restraint had harmed the recovery. Contrary to predictions, the economy boomed in 1978, with the result that unemployment fell to 6 percent—but consumer prices rose by 9 percent. From then on Carter adhered consistently and with increasing determination to a tight budgetary policy.

The 1979 *Economic Report of the President* declared that

efforts to reduce joblessness below 6 percent would result in unacceptably high inflation. This indicated that Carter felt no serious commitment to implement the full-employment provisions of the Humphrey-Hawkins Full Employment and Balanced Growth Act of 1978, which had been enacted in greatly amended form, giving the president considerable discretion to modify its targets according to economic circumstances. The new emphasis on fiscal stringency displeased liberal Democrats. Even within the administration, Vice-President Walter Mondale and Secretary of Health, Education and Welfare Joseph A. Califano were critical of domestic spending cuts. More seriously, Senator Edward Kennedy of Massachusetts established himself as the leading spokesman for dissident liberals through his charges that administration budget policy constituted a repudiation of the Democrats' historic mission to be the party of full employment and social compassion. The dispute was a major factor in prompting Kennedy to run against Carter for the 1980 Democratic presidential nomination. Though his challenge ended in decisive defeat, this was largely due to personal failings, not to lack of support for his views among the party faithful.

Success in the battle against inflation might have silenced the president's critics, but on this front things got worse rather than better. The United States suffered double-digit inflation in consecutive years in 1979–1980 for the first time since World War I. In response the Carter administration trod even harder on the antiinflation brakes. With its support, the Federal Reserve adopted a policy of monetary restraint in late 1979. The 1980 *Economic Report of the President* announced plans to move fiscal policy in the same direction. Expenditure growth was to be curtailed with a view to reducing the projected budget deficit from $40 billion in FY 1980 to $16 billion in FY 1981, and a balanced budget was scheduled for FY 1982. In spite of growing popular demand for tax relief against the effects of inflation, tax reduction was to be deferred until the deficit was eliminated. Even this did not go far enough for the Wall Street money markets, which wanted more rapid progress toward a balanced budget as a mark of resolve to conquer inflation. The consequent fall in bond prices persuaded Carter to revise his budget estimates to eliminate the deficit in FY 1981 by means of spending cuts and the introduction of revenue-raising measures, such as an oil import fee. In addition, selective controls were imposed on credit card usage as a means of restraining consumer buying. The combined effect of these actions was to tip the economy into recession in mid-1980.

This policy-induced downturn occurred too late to exert deflationary pressure before the 1980 elections. As a result, Carter faced the voters with the worse preelection economic record of any president since Herbert Hoover. In conditions of rising unemployment, falling real income, and galloping inflation, it was not surprising that he became the first elected incumbent of the postwar era to be defeated in his bid for a second term. In 1980 two-thirds of voters whose main concern was inflation supported Republican presidential candidate Ronald Reagan, as did just over half of those whose main concern was unemployment. More than any other factor, including the Iranian hostage crisis, economic failure destroyed Carter's presidency. His budgetary policy contributed substantially to his landslide defeat, partly because it was based on dubious assumptions about the relationship between deficit spending and inflation, and partly because it undermined the political economy that had sustained Democratic electoral success for so many years.

As the following table shows, Carter's insistence on a link between deficits and inflation is not borne out by statistical evidence. In FY 1974 the smallest deficit of the first half of the 1970s coincided with the highest inflation rate, and the reverse occurred in FY 1972. The deficit grew substantially from FY 1975 onward, but the increase measured in constant dollars was much smaller than the rise in inflation. Deficit growth was closely related to the relatively high unemployment levels of 1975–1980. Measured in full-employment terms, the Carter era deficits (FY 1978–1981) were smaller on average than those of the Nixon era (FY 1971–1975). It is hard to believe that a full-employment deficit of $2.4 billion in FY 1979 could generate double-digit inflation at a time when GNP was $2.7 trillion. Moreover, the Carter deficits

THE DEFICIT (ON- AND OFF-BUDGET COMBINED) AND INFLATION, FY 1971–1981

| Fiscal Year | Deficit Current $ (billions) | Deficit 1982 $ (billions) | Deficit as % of GNP | Full-Employment Deficit (billion $) | % Change in CPI |
|---|---|---|---|---|---|
| 1971 | 23.0 | 55.8 | 2.2 | 10.6 | 3.4 |
| 1972 | 23.4 | 53.5 | 2.0 | 8.8 | 3.4 |
| 1973 | 14.9 | 32.0 | 1.2 | 13.6 | 8.8 |
| 1974 | 6.1 | 12.0 | 0.4 | 2.2 | 12.2 |
| 1975 | 53.2 | 93.9 | 3.5 | 22.6 | 7.0 |
| 1976 | 73.7 | 120.9 | 4.3 | 18.7 | 4.8 |
| 1977* | 53.6 | 81.6 | 2.8 | 19.4 | 6.8 |
| 1978 | 59.2 | 84.1 | 2.7 | 20.3 | 9.0 |
| 1979 | 40.2 | 52.7 | 1.6 | 2.4 | 13.3 |
| 1980 | 73.8 | 87.3 | 2.8 | 18.0 | 12.4 |
| 1981 | 78.9 | 84.6 | 2.6 | 0.8 | 8.9 |

Source: *Historical Tables, Budget of the United States Government, 1992*, p. 13, 15; U.S. General Accounting Office, "An Analysis of Fiscal and Monetary Policy," August 31, 1982, p. 35.

*Does not include transition quarter data

averaged only 2.4 percent of GNP, compared with 3.6 percent for the Ford deficits of FY 1976–1977, when inflation was comparatively low.

Monetarist claims that the deficits had to be financed through an inflationary expansion of the money supply were also wide of the mark. By far the major source of funding in the 1970s was public borrowing, not Federal Reserve purchase of Treasury securities. Nor did increased government borrowing crowd out private borrowing and drive up interest rates. The high interest rates of the late 1970s and early 1980s were due to the Federal Reserve's calculated decision to launch an all-out attack on inflation, not to tight credit conditions resulting from deficit growth.

Oil and food price hikes, cost-of-living wage increases that were not tied to productivity gains, and slow productivity growth were the main sources of inflation in the 1970s. The OPEC oil price hike of 1979 was the single most significant cause of inflation in the final Carter years. Supply shocks of this nature produced cost-push inflation rather than the kind of demand-led inflation that was attributable to fiscal policy in the late 1960s. A number of respected econometricians have produced data showing that had Carter succeeded in balancing his final budgets, the core inflation rate would have been reduced by less than 1 percent, and the loss of fiscal stimulus would have driven up unemployment. Their evidence indicates that the American economy would have been in even greater difficulties without the deficits of the 1970s.

Carter's hopes of balancing his last budget in FY 1981 were destroyed by the recession and congressional refusal to support all his proposals. Nevertheless, he was nearly successful in balancing it at the full-employment level, just as he had been in FY 1979. A president more committed to his party's traditions would have propagandized the concept of the full-employment budget as the first line of defense for deficit spending. After all, Richard Nixon, a Republican, had shown no qualms about making use of this in the early 1970s, and even the more conservative Gerald Ford had done so in the great recession. But Jimmy Carter's concern about inflation caused him to turn his back on this symbol of fiscal liberalism. When he talked of balancing the budget, it was evident that he had an old-fashioned concept of what this meant rather than one inherited from the new economics of the 1960s.

In some respects Carter may have been unlucky. His economic policy was relatively successful until the oil price shocks of 1979 blew it off course. Thereafter his management of the economy, admittedly in the face of very difficult problems, was ineffective in both economic and political terms. Had Carter remained true to Keynesian principles, he would not have cured inflation, but at least he would not have made it worse. On the plus side, the nation would have been spared the recession of 1980. Carter could then have gone before the electorate as the champion of liberal economic activism. In line with this, he could have stolen Ronald Reagan's thunder by proposing a stimulative tax cut in 1980, as Kennedy and other liberals urged him to do. Instead, his actions and his rhetoric, based on highly questionable assumptions about the inflationary effects of deficits, discredited what his party had long stood for. As a result, the historian James Savage had observed, "any new Democratic budget proposal that added a single dollar to the deficit instantly lost legitimacy on the grounds, supplied by the Democrats themselves, that it helped to cripple the economy." Carter's failure to curb inflation also meant that he did not provide his party with a viable new political economy. All this worked to the advantage of his Republican opponent, who promised to replace the economics of misery with the economics of joy.

### Spend, Spend, Spend!

The political debate over deficits in the 1970s involved more than issues of political economy. Since budgetary records were being broken with amazing regularity, it also encompassed matters of spending control. The deficit, which had surpassed $10 billion only twice before since 1945, fell below this level only once between FY 1971 and FY 1981. The record for the largest deficit, measured in current dollars, was broken no less than four times between FY 1975 and FY 1981, a period when every deficit but one was above $50 billion. Record deficits were a reflection of record spending. It took the United States nearly two hundred years to reach its first $100 billion budget in FY 1962. Over the next twenty years, outlays passed $200 billion in FY 1971, $300 billion in FY 1975, $400 billion in FY 1977, $500 billion in FY 1979, and $600 billion in FY 1981.

In constant-dollar terms, the increase in spending from FY 1971 to FY 1981 was less spectacular and measured only 43 percent. This was actually less than the real increase in spending in the 1940s (143 percent), the 1950s (57 percent), or the 1960s (50 percent). Nevertheless, federal spending reached new peaks in relationship to GNP in the economically stagnant 1970s. Only on two occasions between FY 1947 and FY 1970—in the Korean War budget of FY 1953 and the Vietnam War budget of FY 1968—had expenditure exceeded 20 percent of GNP, but from FY 1971 through FY 1981 the average rate was nearly 21 percent.

Spending growth occurred in spite of institutional efforts to constrain it. In 1970, as part of Nixon's government reorganization program, the Bureau of the Budget was renamed the Office of Management and Budget (OMB) and given a more politicized role to coordinate and police the budget legislative process. Also, far more than any of his predecessors, Nixon refused to spend money appropriated by Congress for specific programs. Other postwar presidents had impounded funding for certain military projects in their capacity as commander-in-chief; Nixon's actions were highly political since they were directed at domestic programs supported by congressional Democrats. In other words, the impoundment power was used to reaffirm the administration's political priorities.

As part of its Watergate-inspired efforts to clip the wings of the imperial presidency, Congress sought to regain the power of the purse through the Budget and Impoundment Control Act of 1974. In addition to limiting presidential impoundment power, this established for the first time a comprehensive congressional budget-making process to rival the president's. Under the old system, budgetary decisions had been made in an uncoordinated manner by a host of standing committees that had jurisdiction over specific elements of taxation, authorization, and appropriation policies. Now the creation of House and Senate budget committees with powers to set binding limits on congressional appropriations and of the Congressional Budget Office to provide technical information and analysis seemingly promised more effective control over spending. Another reform laid down a more rational timetable for budget-making. From FY 1978 onward, the fiscal year was to begin on October 1 rather than July 1. Previously it had often commenced before the congressional appropriations process was complete.

Institutional reform did not prove effective for a number of reasons. The federal budget had become so huge and ongoing commitments so extensive that it was almost impossible to achieve real retrenchment. In essence, budget-making was now an incremental activity. Even with its enhanced powers, the OMB found it difficult enough to resist departmental plans to increase spending and had little chance of enforcing actual cutbacks. Budgetary management was deeply unpopular within the executive branch, since virtually every department wanted to increase its budget. Bureaucratic resistance to the Planning-Programming-Budgeting System, pioneered in the mid-1960s, finally led to its abandonment in 1971. President Carter's plan to introduce zero-based budgeting never got off the ground for the same reason, though its aim of requiring federal departments annually to justify all their spending programs, not just the new ones, would almost certainly have overstretched the OMB's budget review capacity.

Congressional initiatives also failed to achieve expenditure control. Instead of creating a centralized budgetary process, the 1974 reforms had merely grafted new structures onto the existing system. The standing committees traditionally responsible for spending and taxation decisions retained considerable powers. Accordingly, the budget committees tended to accommodate their preferences rather than impose top-down fiscal discipline. This led to the kind of incremental budgeting that had taken hold in the executive branch.

Budget reform also had the unforeseen consequence of encouraging back-door spending through the device of moving a number of loan programs off-budget. The complexity of this process insulated it from public attention in spite of its substantial impact on government finances. During the Carter era the off-budget deficit accounted for nearly a quarter of the total deficit. Congressional committees and executive agencies connived in what was really "creative accountancy" to protect credit programs from budgetary restraints. The Federal Finance Bank (FFB), established in

1973 to limit and coordinate federal loan activity, was given a new and different role to purchase federal loans with money borrowed from the Treasury. Some forty agencies operated credit programs in fields like housing, agriculture, energy, transportation, education, and export assistance. Once the FFB relieved an agency of a loan, it was treated in the budget as if it had been repaid. This made outlays look smaller than they actually were. Although the full liability of the Treasury remained, it had been moved off-budget to the FFB. By 1983 this institution, which had only twelve employees a decade earlier, had assets of $136 billion and had overtaken the Bank of America as the nation's largest bank.

The failure of expenditure control in the 1970s also reflected the changing composition of the budget. Defense's share of the federal budget fell from 41.8 percent in FY 1970 to 22.7 percent in FY 1980. By contrast, the combined share of human resource and physical resource programs (including agriculture) rose from 49.2 percent to 65.7 percent in this period. Budgetary restraint was now much more difficult to achieve than in the days when defense spending was paramount. This was partly because of the political popularity of domestic programs that benefited millions of voters, and partly because outlays on many entitlement programs were indexed to inflation.

The major expansion of domestic spending occurred in human resource programs, whose share of the budget rose from 38.5 percent (7.6 percent of GNP) in FY 1970 to 53.4 percent in FY 1981 (12.1 percent of GNP). As in the 1960s, however, there was an imbalance between outlays on retirement and Medicare programs for the aged and public assistance for the poor. Spending on the latter rose only from 1 percent of GNP in FY 1970 to 1.7 percent in FY 1981. Much of the human resource expansion occurred during the period of divided government from 1969 to 1977, when Republicans occupied the White House and the Democrats controlled Congress. The consequent explosion in social welfare costs effectively precluded the introduction of new programs to redress the balance of aid between the poor and the elderly after the Democrats regained the presidency.

Hoping to build a new Republican electoral majority with the votes of blue-collar families, Nixon joined with congressional Democrats to increase Social Security benefits on no less than four occasions and provide for automatic cost-of-living adjustments from 1974 onward. Cooperation between the two branches was less when it came to public assistance, but spending on Aid to Families with Dependent Children, food stamps, and supplemental security income still rose significantly in the early 1970s. The Republican drive for antiinflation budgetary restraint in the mid-1970s resulted in greater conflict with congressional Democrats over these programs. The Democrats won this battle, but their success served only to stabilize rather than increase current spending levels. Constrained by the stagnant economy and the spiraling deficit, the Democrats bickered among themselves over the issue of public assistance expansion in the late 1970s. Jimmy Carter's plans for the introduction of compulsory national health insurance and a guaranteed-income welfare program came to nothing because of opposition from liberal Democrats for being too cost-conscious and from many moderate and conservative Democrats for being too costly. As a result, the gap between Social Security and welfare widened during his presidency.

The momentum established in the 1960s also generated a substantial expansion of physical resource outlays, particularly for environmental protection, transportation, and community development. Federal grants to the states (excluding transfer

payments for individuals) doubled in real terms from FY
1970 to FY 1977. Physical resource expenditure occasioned
more partisan controversy than social welfare. Both Nixon
and Ford regularly resorted to their veto power in a vain bid
to hold the line against Democratic initiatives. They had
more success in promoting the New Federalism program of
stringless grants and block grants to give states greater
freedom to decide how federal aid should be spent, but this
did not enhance the cause of economy. In effect the Republican
presidents achieved a limited trade-off that entailed a lesser
degree of federal control over grants in return for an
expansion of federal spending. The nonwelfare domestic
budget continued to grow in the late 1970s in spite of
conflict between the White House and Congress. Carter's
determination to finance spending growth in priority areas
through retrenchment in other programs led to conflict with
his own party. Though he succeeded in slowing the rate of
spending growth, congressional Democrats would not support
his demands for real cutbacks in physical resource programs.

The domestic expansion of the 1970s was financed from
two sources: one was the budget deficit, the other—at least
in the Nixon-Ford era—was the shrinkage of the defense
budget. Defense's share of total spending fell by almost half
over the decade as a whole, and defense outlays declined in
real terms by a third from FY 1970 through FY 1976.
America spent less in constant-dollar terms on defense in FY
1976 than it had done in any year since FY 1951. Outlays
began to rise again in the late 1970s, adding to the difficulties
of deficit control. Yet, they were still lower in real terms in
FY 1981 than in FY 1965, the last budget before the
Vietnam War.

The waning of America's involvement in Vietnam and its
final withdrawal after the 1973 peace settlement provided

the impetus for defense contraction. The reduction of post-Vietnam global commitments envisaged by the Nixon Doctrine of 1969 was another factor. Vietnam had also led many Democrats to question cold war doctrines of national security that went hand-in-hand with big defense budgets. Their support for global containment of communism gave way to new foreign policy concerns of peace, arms control, and human rights. In line with this, the Democratic platform in the presidential elections of 1972 and 1976 called for big cuts in military spending. Meanwhile, Republicans continued to argue the case for strong defense. The decline of partisan consensus was reflected in the defense appropriation bills for FY 1970–1975, which averaged almost $4 billion a year less than the president wanted. Congressional economies of this scale were unprecedented in the cold war era. The 1974 budget reforms also facilitated military retrenchment. With Congress now empowered to establish budgetary priorities, defense was more vulnerable to cutbacks, as it had to compete with politically popular domestic programs and was more easily controllable than inflation-indexed entitlements. As a result, some $7 billion was cut from Ford's defense request in the first postreform budget of FY 1976.

Eight consecutive years of military cutbacks came to an end in the last Ford budget. Defense spending rose by .5 percent in FY 1977, a small but symbolically important change. By now there was mounting concern, fueled by the release of separate assessments of U.S. military power by the Congressional Research Service and the Central Intelligence Agency, that America was in decline relative to the Soviet Union. The renewal of cold war tensions in the late 1970s swung the political pendulum further toward defense expansion. Soviet adventurism in the Horn of Africa, the 1979 Soviet invasion of Afghanistan, and setbacks for the U.S. in

Nicaragua and Iran all contributed to a return to defense concerns. In particular, America's seeming impotence in the Iranian hostage crisis of 1979–1980 intensified concern that the nation had to rebuild its power. According to the polls, the number of Americans who felt that too little was being spent on defense doubled between 1977 and 1980.

Despite calls for reduced military spending in the 1976 Democratic platform, the Carter administration and congressional Democrats moved ever closer to the Republican position on defense in the late 1970s. In FY 1980 he proposed a 3 percent real increase for military programs in a budget that sought zero growth in total spending. His FY 1981 budget plan called for an even larger defense increase and a real cut in nondefense. Its projections of sustained growth in military spending into the mid-1980s to reestablish U.S. superiority over the Soviet Union laid the foundations for the Reagan defense program. In fact, the Democratic-controlled Congress voted bigger military appropriations than Carter wanted for both FY 1980 and FY 1981—but refused to make compensatory domestic cutbacks. In essence, though there was widespread agreement among Democrats that the defense budget was inadequate, there was no corresponding consensus that other budgetary goals should be sacrificed to remedy this.

### TAX TROUBLES

Tax receipts also reached record levels in the 1970s, rising from $193 billion in FY 1970 to $517 billion in 1981, a real increase of 28 percent. Federal revenues averaged 18.6 percent of GNP in this period, compared with 18.2 percent in the 1960s and 17.5 percent in the 1950s. Nevertheless, the growing deficit showed that the close approximation sustained since World War II between spending and taxation levels had broken down in the 1970s. Economic growth had hitherto saved policymakers from having to increase taxes to balance the budget. Indeed a buoyant economy had made it possible to increase revenues through cutting taxes, as had been demonstrated in 1964. The stagnant, inflation-prone economy of the 1970s created a more difficult environment for the making of tax policy. Now revenue-raising concerns clashed with the need for antirecession tax cuts and for measures to provide relief from "bracket creep," caused by inflation pushing taxpayers into higher tax brackets without an equivalent increase in their real income. In these circumstances it was hardly surprising that tax policy was characterized by confusion, contradiction, and indiscipline.

The breakdown of policymaking structures that had given coherence to tax policy made matters worse. Presidential dominance of fiscal policy since the 1930s had generally ensured that tax policy was broadly in line with budgetary strategy. But the post-Watergate decline of the presidency was paralleled by growing congressional assertiveness on taxes. All the major tax measures from 1975 onward were more the work of the legislature than the executive. The congressional policymaking process had itself undergone change in the mid-1970s. Previously, the House Ways and Means committee, the dominant voice in the making of tax legislation, had promoted policy stability through its preference for balanced budgets over tax reduction. But its influence was undermined by institutional reforms that sought to clip the wings of the standing committees and their powerful chairmen and to democratize decision-making. As a result, tax policy became more susceptible to change and more responsive to the pressures of organized interests.

The various income tax bills enacted in the Nixon-Ford-

Carter years highlighted the broken nexus between spending and taxation. In a period of escalating deficits, only the 1969 tax reform was intended to increase revenue at the time of passage. All the other measures were meant to reduce tax rates. In spite of this, the tax burden grew heavier rather than lighter. The share of aggregate personal income paid in direct individual taxes by Americans rose from 14.4 percent in 1970 to 15.7 percent in 1980. So it was hardly surprising that politicians were reluctant to risk the wrath of hard-pressed taxpayers by enacting budget-balancing tax increases.

The explanation for the paradox of a shrinking tax base and a rising tax burden was straightforward enough. Personal tax cuts were accompanied by regular increases in Social Security taxes to pay for the benefit increases and cost-of-living adjustments legislated in the early 1970s. In fact, the 1977 Social Security tax increase was the largest peacetime tax increase to date in American history. Meanwhile, bracket creep rapidly eroded the effects of the various personal tax cuts enacted in the 1970s, particularly as inflation accelerated in the second half of the decade. According to congressional estimates, income tax reductions contained in the 1978 tax reform, the most important tax measure of the Carter era, were offset for virtually all income groups by the effects of inflation and higher Social Security contributions.

Tax equity was also an important issue in the 1970s, but the effect of tax policy was to erode rather than improve progressivity. If the tax rates extant in 1967 had simply been sustained and adjusted for inflation, low-income taxpayers would have paid considerably less in taxes and high-income taxpayers considerably more. Social Security tax hikes were one reason for decreased progressivity. In FY 1977–1981 social insurance taxes constituted 30 percent of federal income, more than double the share of corporate income taxes. The increase in "tax expenditures"—the euphemism for loopholes, deductions, exclusions, and credits—also eroded progressivity.

In 1967 tax expenditures numbered fifty (some, like the oil-depletion allowance, dated back to the 1920s), and the revenue loss resulting from them was equivalent to a quarter of total budget receipts. By 1981 tax expenditures exceeded one hundred and entailed a revenue loss of $230 billion, approximately two-fifths of total federal receipts. This had occurred in spite of the determination of some Democrats to close tax loopholes and create a fairer system. Egged on by tax lobbyists, however, most members of Congress regarded tax expenditures as a useful means of counterbalancing the effects of inflation.

Tax loopholes did indeed benefit a huge number of groups, since they allowed such things as mortgage interest deductions, state and local tax deductions, and exclusions for employer-provided pension-plan contributions, insurance premiums, and health benefits. For obvious reasons tax expenditures were (and still are) very popular with the public. But they were regressive rather than progressive. Tax loopholes offer the most benefits to people in upper-income brackets who have the most income to offset. For the vast majority of taxpayers, the effect of tax expenditures was to reduce tax liabilities in proportion to the amount of taxes that they paid.

Paradoxically, the most progressive tax legislation of this period was the 1969 tax reform, promoted by a Republican administration. The most regressive measure was enacted in 1978 when the Democrats controlled both the White House and Congress. This was not the intention of Jimmy Carter, who had promised in the 1976 election campaign to improve the equity of a tax system he called "a disgrace to the human race." But Congress converted his plan to eliminate business loopholes into a measure that lowered capital gains taxes and gave three-quarters of its tax reductions to the wealthiest 2 percent of the nation's taxpayers. Speaking for scandalized liberals, Edward Kennedy proclaimed this "the worst tax legislation approved by Congress since the days of Calvin Coolidge and Andrew Mellon."

Whatever the rights or wrongs of the 1978 Revenue Act, its historical significance as the precursor of Ronald Reagan's supply-side experiment is not in doubt. The final form of the legislation owed much to the lobbying activities of big business, which demanded tax cuts to stimulate capital investment. Such supply-side thinking was also taking hold of the Republican party. The Ford administration's proposals for business tax cuts had been a move in this direction. A more radical measure, based on the theories of University of Southern California economist Arthur Laffer, was advocated in 1977 by a group of Republican congressmen led by Representative Jack Kemp of New York and Senator William Roth of Delaware. This called for a 30 percent cut in marginal tax rates for individuals over a three-year period in order to boost productivity, stimulate investment, and generate high economic growth. Though rejected by Congress, the Kemp-Roth proposal was adopted by Republican presidential candidate Ronald Reagan as the centerpiece of his economic recovery program.

The tax-cutting legislation of 1978 was also enacted against the background of a populist revolt against taxes that gave legitimacy to the emergent fiscal conservatism. The rebellion was focused against state property taxes, which had risen sharply as inflation pushed up property values. It began when California voters gave approval by a two-to-one margin to Proposition 13, a ballot initiative to reduce assessments, limit property taxes, and prevent the easy passage of new taxes. The movement quickly spread, leading to the imposition of some kind of limitation on property taxes in nearly half the states over the next seven years. Resentment of high property taxes did not necessarily equate with demands for reduction of state government spending. Since many states, notably California, operated large budget surpluses, voters had reason to believe that public services could be maintained on lower taxes. Nevertheless, conservatives were confident that the movement could be converted into a rebellion against big federal government and big federal taxes. Poll findings that some 70 percent of families felt they had reached the breaking point on federal taxes encouraged this belief. According to Ronald Reagan, Proposition 13 "triggered hopes in the breasts of the people that something could be done...a little bit like dumping those cases of tea off the boat in Boston harbor."

The growing saliency of the tax-reduction issue occurred at a time when the gap between federal spending and receipts was widening once more. Jimmy Carter had tried in vain to achieve a balanced budget by conventional means of fiscal restraint. Ronald Reagan, on the other hand, promised to cut taxes and eliminate the deficit. The 1980s would show whether the supply-side revolution could deliver on its promises or whether it was nothing more than voodoo economics.

# 6

# The Age of Excess, 1981–1988

THE 1980S WERE an age of fiscal excess marked by spiraling deficits and a skyrocketing national debt. At the outset of his presidency Ronald Reagan promised to balance the budget by 1984, but his record on deficits proved to be the worst in history. Every Reagan budget was more than $100 billion in the red, and three ran deficits of over $200 billion. Meanwhile, the national debt increased from $914 billion in FY 1980 to $2.7 trillion in FY 1989. Budgetary policy changes in the shape of large tax cuts and big defense spending did much to produce the chasm between federal income and outlays. Deficit and debt expansion also became interlinked in a vicious circle. As the federal government's borrowing needs rose, so did its interest repayments, whose annual costs exceeded the size of the deficit by the end of Reagan's presidency. Last but not least, the politics of divided government played a part in shaping the budgetary history of the Reagan era. A Republican president would not sacrifice tax reduction for the sake of a balanced budget, neither would congressional Democrats yield on their spending priorities.

## REAGAN REVOLUTION

"In our present crisis," Ronald Reagan declared in his 1981 presidential Inaugural Address, "government is not the solution to our problems; government is the problem." These words prefaced what many commentators would dub the Reagan Revolution—the attempt to reverse the half-century-long trend of federal government expansion. To Reagan, the most conservative president since Herbert Hoover, big government lay at the root of America's economic problems because it discouraged individual incentive, private enterprise, and wealth creation. To remedy this, he promised a government that spent less, taxed less, and lived within its means. But as the deficit statistics in the table below indicate, the revolution that the federal budget underwent during his presidency was not the one he had anticipated.

Reagan's deficits were revolutionary in three respects. First, their size in current-dollar terms was unprecedented. In constant-dollar terms they were smaller than those of World War II but were still substantially bigger than all but one of the record peacetime deficits of the 1970s. The exception was the recession-affected FY 1976 deficit, which came close to matching Reagan's smallest deficits.

THE REAGAN DEFICITS, FY 1982–1989

| Fiscal Year | Deficit current $ (billions) | Deficit constant 1982 $ (billions) | Deficit as % GNP |
|---|---|---|---|
| 1982 | 127.9 | 127.9 | -4.1 |
| 1983 | 207.8 | 199.2 | -6.3 |
| 1984 | 185.3 | 171.5 | -5.0 |
| 1985 | 212.3 | 190.6 | -5.4 |
| 1986 | 221.2 | 193.9 | -5.3 |
| 1987 | 149.7 | 128.0 | -3.4 |
| 1988 | 155.1 | 128.4 | -3.2 |
| 1989 | 153.4 | 121.9 | -3.0 |

Source: *Historical Tables, Budget of the United States Government, Fiscal Year 1992*, p. 17.

Second, the Reagan deficits were historically large in relation to what the nation as a whole produced and earned. They averaged 4.7 percent of GNP, compared with less than 1 percent for the FY 1950–1969 period (which encompassed both the Korean and Vietnam wars) and 2.2 percent for the FY 1970–1981 era (when the economy experienced stagflation). Even in the Depression era of the 1930s, New Deal deficits had averaged only 3.5 percent of GNP.

Lastly, the Reagan deficits were revolutionary because of the economic circumstances of the 1980s. Roosevelt, Truman, and Eisenhower had used unbalanced budgets to combat recession. The Kennedy-Johnson administrations had broken new ground by running small deficits during periods of modest economic growth. But Reagan operated huge deficits at the high point of the longest economic recovery of the postwar period. The FY 1984–1988 deficits were not the cyclical products of temporary economic conditions but were structural elements of the budget that existed in spite of high employment.

The budget was already in the red when Reagan took office. Although the Carter administration's final budget plan projected a balance between outlays (including off-budget spending) and receipts of FY 1983, this was based on excessively optimistic assumptions about revenue growth. Had Reagan maintained his predecessor's budget program, he would certainly have had to operate deficits, but these would have been comparatively small ones. The runaway deficits of the 1980s resulted from changes in budgetary policy that he initiated. As such, it is fair to label these deficits as Reagan's deficits.

The most important of Reagan's budget policy innovations was the Economic Recovery Tax Act (ERTA) of 1981. This was by far the largest tax cut in American history, dwarfing those of 1948, 1964, and 1975. It included a one-step lowering of the top marginal tax rate from 70 percent to 50 percent, a 23 percent across-the-board cut spread over three years for all other marginal tax brackets, the indexing of the personal tax structure to inflation in order to eliminate bracket creep, and business tax reductions in the shape of accelerated depreciation allowances and investment credits.

In lobbying for the enactment of the ERTA, Reagan often cited the Kennedy-Johnson tax cut of 1964 as proof that lowering taxes would boost economic growth and thereby generate increased revenues for federal coffers. But the earlier measure had been inspired by a Keynesian desire to stimulate consumer demand. By contrast, the Reagan measure was based on the Kemp-Roth supply-side tax reduction proposal, which had gained support among Republicans in the late 1970s. Its assumptions about the economic benefits and revenue-generating potential of supply-side tax cuts proved to be seriously flawed. In addition to these doctrinal problems, contradictions within the administration's economic program and compromises made to secure congressional enactment of the ERTA compounded the harmful consequences of tax reduction for deficit expansion.

Both Keynesian and supply-side economists were in general agreement that underinvestment was the root cause of the low productivity and lack of international competitiveness that bedeviled the U.S. economy, but they prescribed different cures for this. True to the teaching of Keynes that the expectation of profits was the chief determinant of new investment, and that profitability depended on full employment, his disciples advocated a fiscal policy to stimulate aggregate demand and thereby boost jobs. By contrast, supply-side doctrine regarded investment incentives to increase the supply of goods and services produced by the economy as the best remedy for stagflation. Supply-siders blamed America's economic problems on high taxes above all else. In their view, people were deterred from working harder and saving more of their money for investment purposes because too large a proportion of their potential gains would be taken away by government. As a result, productivity and economic growth were retarded, and inflation was encouraged. In support of this argument, the "Laffer curve," conceived by University of Southern California professor Arthur Laffer, sought to demonstrate that above a certain point the tax rate produced diminishing revenues because it was a disincentive to economic activity.

Supply-side theory contradicted the traditional Republican insistence that balanced budgets should be achieved through reductions in spending. According to supply-sider Paul Craig Roberts, who became assistant treasury secretary for economic policy in the Reagan administration, the deficit was "a residual of the economy's performance . . . [and] would gradually be eliminated by economic growth." Such thinking had something in common with the liberal doctrines of the early 1960s. Like the new economists, supply-siders believed that tax cuts held the key to economic growth. Indeed, they regarded the 1964 tax reduction as proof of their own doctrinal pudding. Although the economic expansion of the 1960s was regarded by Keynesians as being consumption-led, the supply-siders claimed it was the result of enhanced saving and investment activity, encouraged by lower taxes.

The supply-side diagnosis had several shortcomings. The Laffer curve hypothesized about the tax rate in the singular, but there were many tax rates, encompassing personal, payroll, business, excise, and state and local taxes. More seriously, neither Laffer nor his supporters could say what the ideal tax rate should be to encourage incentive and generate additional revenues. This rendered the value of his formula dubious at best. The assumption that tax cuts would encourage people to work harder and save more was also questionable. Different people would respond to tax reduction in different ways. Some would spend more in preference to saving, and some would work less in order to have more leisure time.

Most seriously, supply-side doctrine did not address the issue of what investment the economy needed most. It failed to recognize the significance of investment expenditure by government to modernize the nation's infrastructure. In the 1980s the nations that enjoyed the highest rates of productivity growth were those with the best records of public-sector investment in physical capital projects (such as roads, bridges, rail networks, and water and sewage systems) and human capital (education and training to improve the quality of the work force). In terms of private underinvestment, the most serious shortfall in the U.S. economy was in tools and equipment. The revitalization of productivity required this to be remedied, but the most significant investment expansion in the 1980s was in office buildings and shopping centers. To its critics, the supply-side experiment did little to spur real economic growth because it did not target tax incentives at productive investment. Instead, its main achievement was to leave the United States overendowed with the categories of private capital that the economy least needed.

Despite the adoption of the Kemp-Roth formula, Reagan and his economic advisers did not accept supply-side doctrine as the one true faith. The president's own belief in the virtues of tax reduction rested more on personal experience than economic theory. During his heyday as a Hollywood film star in the late 1940s and early 1950s, Reagan found himself in the 94 percent marginal tax bracket if he made

more than four movies a year. This convinced him of a
universal truth: the more government took in taxes, the less
incentive people had to work—whatever their job. To others
in the administration, supply-side doctrine was simply a
convenient excuse for tax cuts. This was a new version of the
1920s "trickle-down theory," that big cuts in the top rates of
taxation paid by corporations and the wealthy were the best
way to boost the economy. The benefits of growth were
expected to work their way down eventually to every economic
group in society. As Office of Management and Budget
(OMB) director David Stockman later admitted, "I've never
believed that just cutting taxes will cause output and
employment to expand....It's kind of hard to sell 'trickle
down,' so the supply-side formula was the only way to get a
tax policy that was really 'trickle down.'" Meanwhile, others
among the president's advisers contended that monetarist
solutions alone could defeat inflation, even though high
interest rates were inconsistent with the aim of enhancing
productivity, investment, and growth.

The Program for Economic Recovery, unveiled in February
1981, reflected the disparity of opinion within the administration. Among other items, it proposed tax reduction to
expand the economy, but also monetary restraints to ensure
that economic growth did not fuel inflation. It was assumed
that tax reduction would be the quickest-acting part of the
program and that a strongly growing economy would generate
sufficient additional revenues to balance the budget at the
lower rate of taxation by FY 1984. In fact, monetary restraint
made itself felt ahead of fiscal stimulus. The White House's
agreement to reduce the amount of tax reduction in the first
year in order to win congressional approval of the ERTA
was partly to blame for this. More significantly, the Federal
Reserve, in yet another demonstration of its independence,

slowed the rate of money supply growth far in excess of the target rates anticipated by the administration. Under the leadership of Paul Volcker, this body was determined to put an end to 1970s-style high inflation. It succeeded, but at the cost of plunging the economy in late 1981 into the worst recession since the 1930s. The result was an automatic decline in tax revenues that made nonsense of the administration's fiscal calculations and launched the series of record deficits. The United States operated its first $100 billion deficit in FY 1982 and its first $200 billion deficit in the following year.

Reducing the first portion of tax reduction was not the only concession needed to secure enactment of the ERTA. Although Republicans had won control of the Senate in the 1980 elections for the first time since 1954, Democrats were still the majority party in the House of Representatives. Democratic congressional leaders contended that the Reagan tax cuts were skewed toward business and the wealthy and would aggravate rather than alleviate the deficit problem. They called instead for proportional tax reduction favoring lower- and middle-income groups. To widen the political appeal of the administration measure, the Republican-controlled Senate Finance Committee formulated an amendment that indexed the individual tax structure to inflation from FY 1985 onward. This was immensely popular with the public because it protected every taxpayer from the kind of bracket-creep that had caused such misery in the 1970s. Nevertheless, this change made the revenue loss from the ERTA much greater than the administration had anticipated. The economy rose out of recession in 1983, but inflation no longer produced a revenue dividend to swell federal coffers at the peak of the recovery cycle.

An evaluation of the policy achievements of the ERTA

depends upon one's outlook. On the plus side it restored the stability and proportionality of middle-class tax structures, which inflation had eroded in the 1970s. By 1979 some three-quarters of all joint tax returns were subject to marginal tax rates of 28 percent or more, compared with only one-sixteenth of joint returns in 1965. But increases in Social Security and energy taxes had eliminated the benefits of tax reduction for many middle- and low-income families. According to the Congressional Budget Office, only the top tenth of income earners saw their effective federal tax rate (the composite of all federal taxes) fall between 1977 and 1988; the large majority of families in the lower half of the income distribution saw theirs rise. Defenders of Reagan's tax record insisted that the lowering of tax rates would facilitate the closure of tax shelters and loopholes, thereby deterring tax avoidance by businesses and high-income earners. But the revenue lost in FY 1992 as a result of tax expenditures that benefited corporations and individuals was estimated at $374.9 billion. This figure was equivalent to 65.5 percent of personal and corporation income tax receipts in the previous year.

The 1981 tax cuts did not perform the promised economic miracles. Supply-siders could argue that their prescription was never properly applied, since it was distorted by interest rate hikes in 1981–1982 and by phased rather than immediate introduction of tax reduction. But economic growth from 1981 through 1988 was impressive only in comparison with the late 1970s. Overall the economy grew at a faster rate in the 1960s and 1970s than in the 1980s. Unemployment was lower in the 1980s than in the Carter era, but it was higher than the average rate for the 1945–1973 period. The real value of wages, which had begun to stagnate in the 1970s, continued to decline in the Reagan years. Only by having more than one wage earner were most families able to boost their income. Trickle-down theory also failed to work in practice. More people lived in poverty at the end of the Reagan era than at the beginning. The number of "hyper-poor," those who lived on cash income amounting to less than half the official poverty level, rose by 45 percent. Tax reduction also failed in its stated aim to boost savings and investment. The net savings rate in relation to national income fell from 7.8 percent in 1979 to 2 percent in 1987. Gross investment, which had averaged 18.8 percent of GNP in the economically troubled years of 1974–1980, declined to 17 percent of GNP in 1981–1991.

The ERTA's impact on the budget was its greatest failing. According to OMB statistics it resulted in a total revenue loss of $643.6 billion in FY 1982–1986. The shortfall rose dramatically after tax rates became subject to inflation indexing in FY 1985. In FY 1986 the revenue loss attributable to the ERTA was $209.8 billion, which nearly equaled the budget deficit of $212.3 billion. It could be argued that this was a worthwhile price to protect individuals from the unfair burden of having to pay a higher percentage of their income in taxes just because inflation was occurring. On the other hand, there were better means of ensuring tax fairness than the ERTA. Whatever one's views, tax indexation surely increased the problems of deficit control. In the past, if tax cuts generated an excessive loss of revenue, the effects were only temporary because bracket-creep would soon boost receipts. As a result of the ERTA, the only way to eliminate a revenue shortfall was through an explicit tax increase enacted by Congress. This was not a nettle that many politicians were anxious to grasp, since voters had a tendency to take revenge on those who raised their taxes.

The continued expansion of federal spending also nourished

the Reagan-era deficits. The painless formula for budget balancing that Reagan had proffered in the 1980 campaign consisted not only of tax reduction to boost revenues but also the elimination of domestic program waste and welfare fraud to allow for increased defense spending. A recognition that gain required pain soon intruded into the new administration's budget plans. Congressman David Stockman's memorandum "Avoiding a GOP Economic Dunkirk" made such a strong impression on the Reagan transition team that it won him appointment as OMB director. In this he argued: "The preeminent danger is that an initial economic package that includes the tax cuts but does not contain decisive, credible elements on matters of policy control, future budget authority reduction and a believable plan for curtailing the government's massive direct and indirect credit absorption will generate pervasive expectations of a continuing 'Reagan inflation.'" Stockman insisted that the deficit had to be eliminated to assuage Federal Reserve fears about inflation and forestall high interest rates that would destroy hopes of an economic boom. In his view, the dilemma of how to cut taxes, increase defense spending, and still balance the budget could only be resolved by huge cuts in domestic expenditures. As Stockman soon discovered, this was much easier said than done.

The OMB had to find economies in programs whose combined outlays represented only some 17 percent of total spending. This was largely because Reagan exempted defense and Social Security entitlement programs from retrenchment. In addition, interest payments on the national debt were an untouchable obligation. Working feverishly to have its plans ready for the launch of the Program for Economic Recovery, the OMB came up with specific proposals to cut $9 billion from the FY 1981 budget inherited from Jimmy Carter and

$40 billion from the FY 1982 plan. But this was not enough to bring the budget into balance by FY 1984, even if the administration's highly optimistic predictions of revenue growth had proved accurate. As a result, the administration's FY 1982 budget plan contained what became known as the "magic asterisk" commitment to make further "unidentified spending reductions" amounting to $74 billion over the FY 1982–1984 period. The assumption that Congress would be willing to support economies on this scale was at best dubious.

Reagan nevertheless won major successes on spending issues during his first year in office. Under the impetus of defense budget increases approved by Congress in 1981, military outlays rose to levels unprecedented in peacetime. By FY 1986 defense expenditure was more than 40 percent higher in real terms than in Carter's final budget and was roughly equal to the post-1945 peak levels during the Korean and Vietnam wars. Reagan also won congressional approval for $34 billion in domestic program cuts in the Omnibus Budget Reconciliation Act of 1981. Though less than he wanted, this was a substantially larger reduction than any other president had achieved.

Reagan showed a sure touch in handling the legislature on spending matters in 1981. The bear pit for his program was the Democratic-controlled House of Representatives. On Stockman's advice, Reagan insisted on employing a reconciliation strategy, an unprecedented tactic but permissible under the terms of the Budget and Impoundment Act of 1974, to secure domestic retrenchment. Congress was required to vote on the complete package of cuts before its standing committees deliberated on specific economies. This procedure established tight guidelines for budgetary decision-making that constrained the normal process of congressional bargaining over appropriations. Reagan also employed his media skills to mold public support for his program. Already shaken by the 1980 election results, House Speaker Thomas P. "Tip" O'Neill of Massachusetts decided that congressional Democrats had to give way to a president who appeared to have the country on his side.

But Reagan was unable to repeat this initial success. In late 1981 Stockman urged in vain that the onset of the recession required the administration to modify its fiscal course. To prevent the deficit from going out of control, he recommended that the final phases of the 1981 tax reduction and the next round of defense expansion be deferred. These were issues on which Reagan would not compromise. Instead the president's FY 1983 budget proposal contained a Deficit Reduction Plan that featured further large cuts in domestic programs, efficiency savings to reduce the costs of government, and stricter enforcement of tax collections. This proposal had no chance of enactment. Amid the worst recession in fifty years, the Democrats had less cause to worry about Reagan's popularity. With high unemployment certain to be an issue in the forthcoming midterm elections, many Republicans were also reluctant to fund military expansion through further domestic retrenchment. "We have a $100 billion increase for defense over three years as we're cutting social programs," complained Republican Senator Dan Quayle of Indiana. "That's totally unacceptable." Congress rejected the president's FY 1983 budget without even taking a formal vote.

This defeat was the final element in the fiscal miscalculations of the Reagan Revolution. The recession had already enlarged the deficit to record proportions. It was also painfully evident that the 1981 tax cuts would not yield the anticipated revenue harvest and that inflation-indexing would act as a drag on receipts when the economy began to recover. Now

Reagan's spending plans had been blown off course too. Domestic retrenchment was nowhere near enough to pay for military expansion. As a result, overall spending was 8.5 percent higher in real terms by the end of Reagan's first term in office than in Carter's final budget. It had also risen from 22.1 percent to 24.3 percent of GNP in this same period. In these circumstances it was hardly surprising that deficit control became one of the dominant political issues of the mid-1980s.

### Dealing with the Deficit

The abject failure of Reagan's strategy for balancing the budget led to other efforts to achieve the same ends by different means. None proved entirely successful, but the deficit had been reduced by the time Reagan left office. The most noteworthy achievement was the $70 billion decline in the deficit in FY 1987, the largest drop ever recorded in a single year. Significantly, it was Congress rather than the president who took the lead in trying to get the budget back on track.

Once it became clear that his plan to balance the budget would not work, Reagan began to look around for culprits to blame. Congress and "greedy" special interests became his scapegoats. In his memoirs, Reagan claimed: "Deficits ... aren't caused by too little taxing, they are caused by too much spending. Presidents don't create deficits, Congress does. Presidents can't appropriate a dollar of taxpayers' money; only congressmen can—and Congress is susceptible to all sorts of influences that have nothing to do with good government." Throughout his presidency Reagan called for a constitutional amendment to require balanced budgets and a line-item veto to give the president more control over the allegedly spendthrift legislature. These proposals had no hope of enactment because not enough congressmen in either party were willing to surrender the congressional power of the purse. Though the Republican-controlled Senate adopted the balanced-budget amendment in 1982, the Democratic-controlled House of Representatives easily defeated it.

In reality, neither measure would have offered an effective solution to the nation's budgetary problems. A balanced-budget amendment would have to permit emergency deficits during a recession or a defense crisis, but this flexibility would almost certainly provide loopholes to avoid restraint even in nonemergency circumstances. Nor would mandating a balanced budget provide the formula for achieving one. The Reagan-era deficits were so large that they could only have been eliminated in the short term by drastic action to cut spending, raise taxes, or both. It is difficult to believe that a bipartisan coalition could have been built in support of any of these options in the 1980s. Even in a different political climate, a balanced-budget amendment would probably have limited effect. Fiscal calculation is not a precise science, so it is susceptible to manipulation. Presidents can overestimate revenues to present a balanced budget on paper. Congress can protect spending programs from deficit-reduction measures by moving them off-budget and by massaging trust fund balances. Moreover, a balanced-budget amendment would have its greatest impact on discretionary spending, where political control has already proved effective. Its influence on uncontrollable items—like entitlements, credit programs, and debt repayment—would be slight. For this reason, too, a line-item veto giving the president power to reject separate parts of a spending bill without having to veto the entire measure would have little value as an instrument for balancing the budget.

Some members of Reagan's own administration were contemptuous of his refusal to adopt a more practical approach to deficit control. David Stockman, for example, complained that the president stopped listening, "ignored all the palpable, relevant facts and wandered in circles" when efforts were made to engage him in debate on this issue. Reagan's insistence that domestic spending cuts should bear the main burden of budget balancing made fiscal sense but was politically unrealistic, since retrenchment on this scale stood no chance of winning congressional approval. From a political perspective, however, his strategy was astute. It enabled him to protect his income tax cuts and defense expansion from substantial revision. It placed the onus for deficit reduction on Congress, thus allowing the president to blame the legislature—particularly its Democratic members—for the expansion of the deficit. And it meant that Reagan's posture on the budget was now essentially a defensive one to preserve what he had already achieved. This was a much easier task than building support for a new budgetary policy.

Even had Reagan preferred to keep the initiative, it is doubtful that Congress would have let him. The president's budget had lost credibility with both Republican and Democratic legislators on account of the wildly inaccurate projections in his FY 1982 plan. His use of the reconciliation strategy, a device originally intended to enhance congressional budgetary power, to win approval of his first budget had added insult to injury. For the remainder of Reagan's presidency, every budget plan that he submitted to Congress was pronounced "dead on arrival" and largely ignored. But as past experience had shown, the legislature lacked the discipline to eliminate the deficit by itself. As a result, budgeting became a haphazard, ill-defined process in the Reagan era.

Democratic leaders in Congress sought to transfer the onus for deficit reduction from spending to taxes. Their efforts to repeal the final portion of the ERTA personal tax cuts in 1982 encountered Reagan's unyielding opposition. Opinion polls confirmed that the overwhelming mood in the country was on the president's side. The American people valued lower personal taxes more than a lower deficit. In these circumstances, congressional Republicans and many conservative Democrats rallied in support of Reagan. Nevertheless, a deal was brokered between the White House and congressional leaders of both parties to enhance revenue by raising business taxes. The only opposition to this came from the supply-side faction among the congressional Republicans, led by Jack Kemp. To highlight GOP divisions and to ensure that the Republicans did not portray it as a Democratic tax, Speaker O'Neill refused to back the measure unless the president worked personally for its enactment. "I want him to use that smiley countenance, that sweet-talking voice of his," he declared, "and be as hard-knuckled with his Republicans as he has been along the line." Reagan duly went on television to speak for the bill, but presented it as a tax reform rather than a tax increase.

The Tax Equity and Fiscal Responsibility Act (TEFRA) of 1982 rescinded some of the business tax benefits that Congress itself had written into the ERTA. As such it reduced corporate tax revenue losses from the earlier legislation to levels close to Reagan's original proposal. It also included new taxes in the shape of "user fees" for government services and the elimination of several tax loopholes. TEFRA was expected to net $98 billion in extra revenue in FY 1983–1985.

Congress also agreed on a package of expenditure reductions intended to save a further $30 billion in the same period. Many of these economies were spurious, though, since they included uncontrollable items, such as lower interest payments on the national debt and efficiency savings in government. Energy taxes were also raised in 1982. A big hike in Social Security taxes followed in 1983. In addition, the Deficit Reduction Act of 1984 provided for further closure of tax loopholes and some reduction of tax benefits for business and wealthy individuals, as well as the kind of soft savings on expenditure that had been approved in 1982. The combined effect of all the measures enacted in 1982–1984 was to prevent the budget going $300 billion into the red, which some projections had forecast. This was some crumb of comfort in the face of the still astronomical deficits being incurred.

Further repeal of business tax benefits offered little hope for raising budget-balancing revenues. The only way tax policy could eliminate the deficit was by rescinding the ERTA personal tax cuts. Reagan's landslide reelection in 1984 ensured that this would be kept off the political agenda. Probably the clearest policy difference between the president and his opponent, Walter Mondale, in this contest was over taxation. The Democrat, formerly vice-president in the Carter administration, ran on a platform that promised to reduce the deficit by improving the progressivity of the tax system, clawing back some of the Reagan tax gains for wealthy Americans, and partially deferring inflation-indexing of the tax structure. No modern presidential candidate had previously won election on the basis of a promise to raise personal taxes, and Mondale was no exception. Afterward he ruefully commented, "I taught a whole generation of politicians how to handle the tax issue: to not mention it."

The major change in tax policy in Reagan's second term was revenue-neutral. The Tax Reform Act of 1986 was concerned with fairness. It embodied both the president's populist conservatism and the Democrats' dislike of tax giveaways to the rich. Reagan had long felt that high marginal tax rates were not only a deterrent to economic growth but also an infringement on individual liberties. The 1986 reform addressed his concerns by replacing the existing schedule of individual tax rates with lower rates of 15 percent, 28 percent, and 33 percent. Top-income earners gained a reduction on their current 50 percent rate, but over four million people at the bottom end of the income scale were exempted from paying income tax by reform of the income base. The loss in revenues was to be made up through the elimination of business tax preferences, capital gains allowances, and tax exemptions for the wealthy.

The political impossibility of a substantial tax increase meant that spending had to bear the burden of deficit reduction. The most important initiative on this front was the Balanced Budget and Emergency Deficit Control Act of 1985. This was better known as Gramm-Rudman-Hollings (G-R-H) after the senators who were its main sponsors, conservative Republicans Phil Gramm of Texas and Warren Rudman of New Hampshire, and Democrat Ernest Hollings of South Carolina. The measure appealed to right-wing Republicans because it defined the deficit as bad and set out to eliminate it through spending reductions. G-R-H was also acceptable to liberal and moderate Democrats for several reasons. First, it offered a means to constrain Reagan's defense expansion. Equally important, the Democrats won exemption from its terms for a number of public assistance programs, and the politically sensitive Social Security program was moved off-budget as a guarantee of its untouchability.

G-R-H was a law that reflected the legislature's lack of trust both in itself and the president to deal with the deficit problem of their own free will. It was akin to a dieter who removes food from the house to forestall the temptation of raiding the larder. Phil Gramm himself described G-R-H as "a bad idea whose time has come." The measure established a sliding scale of maximum allowable deficits from FY 1986 through FY 1991. The aim was to reduce the deficit by annual slices of $36 billion until it was eliminated altogether at the end of this period. Whenever Congress and the administration failed to meet the deficit target, the Comptroller General, who headed the General Accounting Office (GAO), would issue a report mandating automatic cuts in spending, drawn in roughly equal amounts from defense and nonexempt domestic programs. The only circumstances in which these automatic provisions would not operate were during war or recession.

The cynicism that inspired G-R-H was well founded since its provisions were routinely flouted. In 1986 the Supreme Court ruled in *Bowsher v Synar* that authority to require spending cuts was an executive prerogative, and that giving this to the GAO, which was an agent of Congress, violated the constitutional separation of powers. After this it was decided that economies could only be instituted through congressional vote and presidential agreement. The practical effect was to make deficit reduction voluntary rather than mandatory.

Reagan's final budget in FY 1989 carried a deficit of $153.4 billion, instead of $72 billion as originally projected by G-R-H. Both the White House and Congress used creative accounting techniques to circumvent the weakened terms of this measure. Even though Democrats had regained control of the Senate in the 1986 elections, they connived with the president's practice of issuing overly optimistic revenue forecasts on which deficit reduction projections were based. Other ploys to avoid making real cuts included putting more programs off-budget, moving expenditures from one fiscal year to the next, and selling national assets to generate one year's income. The huge surplus in the Social Security fund was used to offset on paper part of the deficit in the rest of the budget. More reprehensible was that trust-fund balances in accounts designed to maintain and improve roads and air traffic were not spent in order to make the deficit appear smaller, even though the money was desperately needed for its proper purpose. As one disillusioned congressional aide commented, "Gramm-Rudman just about destroyed credible budgeting. Games have been played before, but I've never seen so many games as this time."

The Wall Street stock market crash of October 1987, which saw $500 billion wiped off the value of shares in a single day, led to renewed concern about the deficit. This plunge was widely attributed to business anxiety about the impact of government borrowing needs on interest rates, capital flows, and the trade balance. In these circumstances the administration agreed to accept a new deficit-reduction plan crafted by congressional Democrats. The Balanced Budget Reaffirmation Act of 1987 revised the G-R-H targets to schedule a balanced budget by FY 1993. It included provision for $5 billion in spending cuts and $23 billion in tax increases. Like G-R-H, this proved to be more window dressing than the real thing. Creative accounting continued to undermine efforts to make true reductions in spending. Though the tax increases did affect individual as well as business taxes, they amounted to little more than tinkering with the system. The basic provisions of the ERTA were left intact. In spite of the 1987 tax hike, tax revenues declined slightly as a percentage of GNP between FY 1987 and FY 1989 because of the effect of inflation-indexing.

This was the final deficit-reduction effort of the Reagan years. Like all the others, it fell prey to the vagaries of divided government. There was little prospect that a Republican administration committed to preserving tax reduction and defense expansion and a Democratic Congress determined to safeguard domestic programs could produce an effective solution to the deficit problem. Recognizing this, both sides agreed in late 1987 to establish a bipartisan National Economic Commission to investigate means of balancing the budget and report after the election of a new administration. It did not require a fiscal expert to see that some sacrifices would be necessary to restore fiscal discipline. Less clear was whether a political consensus on this score would ever be possible.

### Warfare versus Welfare

A core element of the deficit problem was the dispute over spending priorities. Reagan sought to fund the biggest military expansion in peacetime history through domestic retrenchment while Democrats wanted a trade-off that favored social programs over defense. The resulting stalemate between them meant that no framework existed for coordinating defense and domestic programs with revenue levels.

The most famous feature of Reagan's defense buildup was the proposal to develop the Strategic Defense Initiative (SDI). A $1 trillion price tag made this the most expensive new weapons system in history. Originally scheduled for completion in the late 1990s, SDI was to be a space-based defensive shield that would use high-tech lasers to destroy incoming missiles in the event of a nuclear attack on the United States. Star Wars, as SDI was popularly known, and the B-1B strategic bomber represented exceptional cases of new weapons development. The Reagan defense program

mainly entailed the acceleration of development and procurement schedules for existing programs and the expansion
of planned force levels.

There was no basic reformulation of military doctrine in
the 1980s. Instead the Reagan administration's defense
increases were spread broadly among almost every type of
program, both strategic and conventional. Its concern was to
have more of everything. In essence, military power was
equated with the size and growth of the overall defense
budget rather than with superiority in any particular weapons
system. Reagan's early defense budgets put particular emphasis
on investment programs, such as procurement, research and
development, and military production, which laid the seeds
for sustained expansion of outlays in years to come. The
intention was to signal to both friend and foe that the 1970s
retreat from power was over.

Real spending on defense (measured in 1982 dollars) rose
rapidly from its post–Korean War low of $153.6 billion in
FY 1976 to a peacetime record of $230 billion in FY 1985.
This expansion belied the theory that defense spending
should be one of the most stable parts of the budget, since
the concerns of national security tend to be enduring rather
than transitory. The politicization of the defense budget in
the 1970s had made long-term expenditure planning almost
impossible to achieve. The cold war consensus that supported
stable defense spending had given way in the wake of
Vietnam to new political divisions over America's role in
world affairs. Reform of the congressional budget process
had also given the antimilitarist bloc that had emerged
within the Democratic party a powerful leverage over national
security spending. The result was a feast-or-famine approach
to defense as the political balance shifted to and fro between
expansionists and economizers. In this context it is at least

understandable how the military budget mushroomed in the 1980s without due regard for its effect on the deficit. Given the volatility over defense, expansionists felt they had to seize their opportunity to get as much as they could as quickly as possible.

What made the new defense buildup possible was the American public's growing concern that the post-Vietnam retrenchment had allowed the Soviets to gain military superiority. Reagan made this a major issue in his 1980 election campaign. Capitalizing on his landslide victory, he won approval for even bigger defense increases than Jimmy Carter had projected. The defense budget grew in real terms by almost 25 percent in FY 1982–1985 in spite of unprecedented congressional cutbacks in the president's spending requests. In the last three of these budgets $20 billion less on average was authorized for defense than Reagan wanted, but this amounted to mere trimming of the huge expansion that had been set in motion.

The defense program lost momentum in Reagan's second term, during which real growth was only 11.5 percent. By now the political pendulum was swinging back toward the economizers. Public opinion was less fearful about Soviet military power, partly because progress toward nuclear arms reduction pointed to a thaw in superpower relations but mainly because the Reagan buildup had assuaged popular concern about national security. The growing significance of deficit control in the political agenda also weakened support for defense expansion. It was the prospect of renewed trade-offs from defense to domestic programs that induced Reagan to accept G-R-H. This mandated that only half of any automatic spending cuts would come from defense and exempted the SDI from its provisions. The White House feared that a nonformulaic approach to deficit reduction would result in much more severe military retrenchment.

Reagan was less successful in cutting domestic programs than in expanding defense. Physical resource programs, whose outlays were discretionary, proved most vulnerable to his economy drive. Real federal spending in this sector declined by some 25 percent during Reagan's presidency. This represented a reversal of the expansionary trend that had lasted since the mid-1950s. Only agriculture—whose outlays were uncontrollable—resisted this retrenchment. The real reduction of 40 percent in the amount of money that the states received from federal grants-in-aid during the 1980s was probably the best index of Reagan's domestic policy achievement. And a change in the composition of this spending reflected conservative animus against the Great Society. Grants-in-aid for programs tracing their lineage to the 1960s, notably regional development, housing and urban development, and pollution control, took savage cuts. Traditional public works escaped with comparatively light reductions. Nevertheless, federal, state, and local government combined spent only 1 percent of GNP a year on infrastructure projects (like roads, bridges, and sewage and water systems) in the 1980s compared with 3 percent in the 1950s and 1960s. In other words, the cumulative deficit in public infrastructure investment during the Reagan presidency was equal to 16 percent of GNP. To some economists this was the prime cause of slow productivity in the 1980s.

Measured purely in terms of spending, Reagan had far less success in reducing social welfare expenditures. In the aggregate, federal payments for individuals accounted for approximately the same percentage of total budget outlays and GNP at the end of his presidency as at its outset. Again, however, there were important changes in the composition of outlays. Income and health assistance programs for the poor—with the exception of Medicaid—experienced relative decline as a proportion of total spending on human resources. By contrast, Social Security and Medicare rose from less than 50 percent to nearly 60 percent of outlays in this category during the 1980s.

Expenditure control was not a problem insofar as welfare was concerned. The Omnibus Budget Reconciliation Act of 1981 restricted eligibility and reduced benefit formulas for several programs, notably Aid for Families with Dependent Children and food stamps. It also initiated the redirection of public assistance from income maintenance to preparation and training for work, popularly labeled workfare. This trend culminated in the passage of the Family Support Act of 1988.

By contrast, Reagan's proposals for modest reductions in social insurance benefits went down to humiliating defeat in the Senate in 1981. Not even right-wing Republicans dared to risk the enmity of the elderly, who had become an active and potent pressure group. After this, Reagan made little attempt to control the growth of Social Security outlays but concentrated instead on supplying additional revenues to fund present and future needs. There was considerable irony in this. The president who was willing to fight income tax increases to the death did not flinch from introducing Social Security tax increases. As a result the Social Security fund, which had looked dangerously anaemic, was running a healthy surplus by the time he left office. This only served to mask the large deficit that existed for other parts of the budget. In reality, too, the solvency of Social Security had effectively been purchased by the diversion of funds from welfare programs that assisted the nonelderly poor.

### THE REAGAN DEFICITS—MALIGN OR BENIGN?

The political focus on deficit reduction did not signify consensus on the danger of large deficits to the nation's well-being. Political leaders and professional economists held differing views on this score. Perhaps the most remarkable feature of this division was the turnaround that occurred in party opinion. Balanced budgets had once been a staple element in Republican ideology, but Ronald Reagan eventually came to believe that deficits were not necessarily harbingers of economic woe. By contrast, Democrats, the party that had made unbalanced budgets respectable, became fierce critics of the deficit in the 1980s.

The explanation for Reagan's metamorphosis is a simple one: he tolerated unbalanced budgets in order to protect his tax cuts and his military expansion. This meant that he had to refute his once firmly held conviction that deficits were economically harmful. It is hard to believe that Reagan's budgetary statements in the 1980 and 1984 elections were made by the same person. In the earlier campaign he insisted that deficits caused inflation and high interest rates. In 1984 he denied that they were connected and repeatedly emphasized that interest rates and inflation had fallen while the deficit had grown over the previous two years. Others in the administration now sang the same song, notably Treasury Secretary Donald Regan. Those who dared to question the new orthodoxy found their influence eclipsed. CEA chairman Martin Feldstein resigned office in disillusion in 1984, followed the next year by frustrated budget-balancer David Stockman.

Reagan's new line of economic thinking did not mean that he now favored unbalanced budgets. He still disapproved of deficits as political symbols of big government. It was his good fortune that he could have his cake and eat it: he could fulminate against excessive spending on domestic programs as the root cause of unbalanced budgets, while drawing comfort from the knowledge that the huge deficits acted as a constraint on further expansion of the federal government's responsibilities. The 1980s stand out in modern American history for their comparatively little development of new domestic programs. The Democratic party's energy was focused on trying to protect the legacy of the 1960s and 1970s rather than promoting fresh reforms. The deficit problem effectively ruled out a more ambitious agenda.

This was one reason why Democrats turned against unbalanced budgets. They viewed the Reagan deficits as a threat to their party's historic mission to use the powers of government to benefit the less advantaged groups in society. True, congressional Democrats were able to contain Reagan's offensive against existing programs and limit the scope of domestic retrenchment. But they were in no position to launch new spending programs that addressed the social problems of late-twentieth-century America, such as growing drug dependency, AIDS, ghetto violence, the need for better schools, and the poverty that trapped millions in a permanent underclass. As Senator Ernest Hollings remarked in 1984, "[Reagan] not only cuts the programs, but he likes the fact that deficits will keep us Democrats from ever even discussing new programs. If we can ever get that White House again we'll have a hard time restoring the programs and properly funding them. But with those high deficits for years we won't have any chance at all to talk about new programs."

Democrats also viewed the Reagan deficits as an economic malignancy. They made this the major issue in their 1984 presidential campaign and advocated higher taxes as the only possible cure. Democratic candidate Walter Mondale avowed: "We are living on borrowed time. These deficits hike interest rates, clobber exports, stunt investment, kill jobs, undermine growth, cheat our kids, and shrink our future....I mean business. By the end of my first term, I will reduce the Reagan budget deficit by two-thirds." His words signaled the completion of the revolution in the Democratic view on deficits that had commenced in the Carter era.

In the contest for popular support on the deficit issue, Reagan was the undisputed winner. The Democratic castor oil of bigger taxes was deeply unpopular. In the absence of an economic crisis that could be blamed on the deficit, few Americans saw the need for such an unpleasant cure. In fact, surveys conducted at the start of the 1984 campaign by White House pollster Richard Wirthlin found that only 42 percent of respondents knew that the deficit had grown during Reagan's presidency. Other polls showed that Americans did not hold Reagan responsible for the deficit and, what's more, believed he would be more effective than Mondale in reducing it. These views reflected the deep-rooted popular image of the Democrats as the deficit party, which their opposition to the balanced-budget amendment had reinforced. Mondale's strongest issue turned out to be not the deficit but jobs, traditionally the Democrats' best vote-winner. But his appeal to those who worried about unemployment was blunted by his insistence that higher taxation was necessary for the health of the economy.

The Democrats had failed to sell their message to voters. But was it the right one? Were the large deficits as harmful as they claimed? There is no simple answer to these questions. There were "good" deficits and "bad" deficits in the Reagan era. The early deficits fall into the former category, since they were instrumental—along with the relaxation of monetary policy—in lifting the economy out of its deepest recession in fifty years. Accordingly, the giant FY 1983 deficit of $207.7 billion converted into a full-employment deficit of only $53.7 billion (excluding off-budget outlays). The Democratic party's fiscal policy amidst the recession refuted its Keynesian past. Its abortive efforts to repeal the final portion of personal tax cuts and its successful proposal to raise business taxes suggested that deficit control had become more important to it than reducing unemployment.

The Democratic critique made more sense when applied to the Reagan deficits from FY 1984 onward because these resulted from insufficient revenue and excessive spending rather than recession. Even on this score, however, there was no consensus among professional economists. Supply-siders insisted that the second-term deficits were benign and need not be eliminated through tax increases. Some liberal economists took the same view. Robert Eisner of Northwestern University even claimed that the deficit was a statistical illusion. In his opinion, inflation had grossly distorted the size of the nominal deficit, making it appear nearly twice the size of the real or inflation-adjusted deficit. He also sought to distinguish between government spending that was mere consumption of services and what was investment in long-term assets, such as roads, natural resources, and military equipment, which he claimed should not be counted as part of current expenditure. Simply stated Eisner's thesis was that the deficit was really much smaller than it looked. The trouble with this analysis was that for something supposedly small, the deficit caused all too large problems.

The bloated national debt was one harmful consequence of the huge deficits. Like other conservatives, Reagan had long denigrated liberal Keynesianism as a tax-and-spend philosophy. Now he had substituted a political economy of spend-and-borrow. The national debt had risen steadily from $258.7 billion in FY 1945 to $914.3 billion in FY 1980. By FY 1989 it had skyrocketed to $2.7 trillion. Other periods had witnessed massive growth in the national debt, but these were usually associated with American involvement in war. The only peacetime instance was during the Great Depression of the 1930s. The historical circumstances of debt expansion in the 1980s were unique. Also, in contrast to the post-1945 trend, the debt burden grew in the Reagan era at a much faster rate than the economy. In measuring this, the important index is the debt held by the public. It must be borne in mind that a portion of the debt, usually 15 to 20 percent, is held by the government itself in its various trust funds (such as Social Security and highways). The public debt–GNP ratio rose from 29 percent to 45 percent during Reagan's presidency. By the time he left office, the United States confronted a debt burden not seen since the early 1960s, when it was still paying off its World War II borrowings.

Supporters of the "benign deficit" theory responded to this development by asking, "So what?" To them the growth of the national debt was only important if it impaired government creditworthiness, which it patently did not. The U.S. government was not in any kind of financial crisis. In contrast to most individuals who sink into debt, it had no difficulty borrowing more money to pay its bills. Creditors were confident that the federal government could always meet its debt obligations because it had a huge and guaranteed income from tax revenues. Nor was the debt burden in the 1980s by any means the heaviest in modern times. The debt-GNP ratio at the end of the Reagan era was still less than half its level at the end of World War II.

Nevertheless, the accumulation of debt carried costs both for taxpayers and the economy. The most visible of these was the rise in federal interest payments from $69 billion to $169 billion (almost double in real terms) and from 10.1 percent to 14.8 percent of total outlays between FY 1981 and FY 1989. The fastest-growing part of the budget, interest on the public debt became the third largest spending item behind Social Security and defense. By FY 1989 the cost actually exceeded the size of the deficit. Without this albatross around its neck, the United States would in theory have been operating a pay-as-you-go budget. More to the point, soaring interest payment drained fiscal resources away from other areas. In FY 1989 it cost twice as much as the physical resource programs put together.

The Reagan deficits were also intimately connected with the alarming growth in America's international trade deficit during the 1980s. The twin deficits, as some observers labeled them, were interlinked by a chain of economic factors. The first part of this was the collapse of national saving from 7.9 percent of national income in 1980 to 2 percent in 1987. National saving determines what funds the nation has available for investment. It can be defined as the portion of the nation's current earnings that is set aside to provide for the future. One cause of its decline in the 1980s was the fall in household savings, as families loaded up with credit to participate in the postrecession consumer boom. But the major factor was the massive dis-savings (or negative saving) involved in running the Reagan deficits. In effect, federal government borrowing absorbed about two-thirds of all net saving by business and individuals. What remained to finance net private investment was therefore around two cents on each dollar of the nation's earnings, just a fourth as much as in the 1970s.

The collapse of national saving meant that businesses and individuals had to compete for diminished investment funds.

The result was to drive up *real* interest rates, that is the interest rate minus the inflation rate. Nominal interest rates were brought down after the 1981–1982 recession, but real interest rates remained high because inflation was in decline. By contrast, real interest rates were coming down in Western Europe and Japan, where most governments were steadily reducing their budget deficits in relation to national income. As a result, foreign investors increasingly used their savings to buy stocks and bonds, property, and even whole businesses in the United States, where they could now get a better return on their money than at home. In addition, Treasury securities, always popular with foreigners, increased their appeal. Some 15 to 20 percent of the national debt held by the public was funded from abroad in the Reagan era, compared with 10 percent in 1960. This carried significant economic costs. A large national debt funded domestically simply redistributed income in favor of American citizens who purchased government bonds; but payment of interest to foreigners required the transfer of national income out of the country. Meanwhile, American investment abroad dried up because of the insufficiency of national saving. A huge reversal had occurred in the normal directions of capital flows. The effect was to transform the United States from the world's largest creditor nation in 1981 to the largest debtor nation in 1985.

The influx of foreign capital generated an enormous international demand for American currency. The dollar consequently began a startling rise in value against other currencies, making foreign imports cheaper for Americans and American goods dearer abroad. The effect was to widen the trade deficit from $25 billion in 1980 to $170 billion in 1987. Efforts by the United States and its main trading partners to coordinate exchange rate policy helped to reduce the value of the dollar after 1985. But the damage to America's trade position proved more difficult to put right. Though not the bargains they used to be, foreign manufactured goods had established sales outlets and consumer loyalty, which gave them an enduring position in the U.S. market. The trade deficit cost jobs in the manufacturing sector of the American economy. It also mortgaged future national income to foreigners. The United States had to pay for its imports by selling off assets to foreign investors. The returns on these were therefore flowing out of the country instead of being reinvested to boost American productivity.

The Reagan deficits opened up a pandora's box of economic problems. True, there was no day of reckoning in the form of a major economic crisis in the 1980s. The closest that the United States came to this was the stock market crash of 1987, which resulted from declining investor confidence and concern about the possibility of foreign withdrawal of funds from the country. But the deficits of the 1980s weakened the structural foundations of the economy. Reagan's legacy was a rising debt burden, the collapse of national saving, and stagnant investment. Unless corrective action was undertaken by his successors, there was a danger that the next generation of Americans would bear the consequences in the form of slow economic growth, a reduced standard of living, and the decline of U.S. power in the world.

# 7

## Deficit Government: The Present, the Future—and the Past

WORSENING BUDGETARY PROBLEMS forced the United States to face up to fiscal reality in the early 1990s. The deficit, which had started to shrink in the final Reagan years, widened once more. It rose in rapid succession to $221.4 billion in FY 1990, $269.5 billion in FY 1991, and $290.4 billion in FY 1992. The national debt consequently mushroomed from $2.8 trillion in FY 1989 to $4 trillion in FY 1992. These statistics exposed the lie of the deficit-reduction programs concocted in the 1980s. It was now recognized that a more serious effort had to be made to deal with the budget problem. This became the dominant political issue of the post-Reagan era, particularly during the early stages of Bill Clinton's presidency. There was consensus about the need to reduce the deficit but not about how this should be done. A new budgetary agenda was put in place only after prolonged wrangling. Nevertheless, the live now, pay later outlook of the Reagan years finally gave way to the more sober view that regarded deficit reduction as a test of American government's capacity to act in the nation's long-term interest.

## TAMING THE DEFICIT MONSTER

Deficit reduction on the scale required in the early 1990s was a politically risky venture. It could only be done through actions that would have an immediate effect on millions of citizens, namely tax increases and spending cuts. By contrast, the benefits of deficit reduction were more relevant for the future than for the here-and-now and would be less discernible at the micro-level of individuals' lives than at the macro-level of the nation's economy. Strong leadership was therefore required to convert deficit-reduction rhetoric into policy reality, but the American political system militated against this. The separation of powers between president and Congress and the relative weakness of party cohesion multiplied the difficulties of tackling the nation's budget problems. This was underlined when President George Bush encountered far greater difficulty in building bipartisan support of a deficit-reduction package in 1990 than in mobilizing an international coalition to confront Iraqi dictator Saddam Hussein. Similarly, Bill Clinton's budget program came perilously close to defeat in 1994, even though Democrats had comfortable majorities in both houses of Congress.

Nothing demonstrated the propensity of American politics to elevate short-term gain over long-term interest more than the taxation issue. Ronald Reagan's explicit refusal to sacrifice tax reduction for the sake of balanced budgets had sealed his victory in the 1984 presidential election. George Bush nailed his colors to the same mast four years later with his famous pledge, "Read my lips: no new taxes." This was instrumental in his defeat of the Democratic presidential candidate, Governor Michael Dukakis of Massachusetts. But the opportunity to educate the American public about basic fiscal truths had been lost. Ironically, back in the distant days when the two were rivals for the 1980 Republican nomination, it was Bush who had coined the term "voodoo economics" to describe Reagan's claim that lower taxes were the foundation for a balanced budget. As president, Bush soon found himself practicing his own brand of voodoo budgeting.

Bush's first budget plan, presented early in 1989, employed the "smoke-and-mirrors" approach to deficit reduction that had become common since the enactment of the Gramm-Rudman-Hollings (G-R-H) measure. The revised G-R-H targets, agreed in 1987, required the deficit to be kept below $100 billion in FY 1990. To stay within the limit, the executive budget proffered highly optimistic revenue estimates, proposed unspecified spending cuts, and resorted to various accounting gimmicks. Democratic leaders in Congress charged that Bush was simply deferring the day of reckoning, but they failed to produce more constructive deficit reduction proposals of their own. Since neither side wished to be blamed for unpopular measures, both maintained the illusion that real progress was being made in meeting the G-R-H targets. A summit meeting between White House officials and Democratic leaders produced a budgetary agreement, and a bipartisan vote sustained its eventual enactment by Congress. But this cooperation represented the avoidance of difficult choices rather than the resolution of differences for the sake of the long-term common good.

The FY 1991 budget process promised to be a replay of the previous year's until events dictated otherwise. Bush produced another smoke-and-mirrors budget plan that kept within the G-R-H maximum deficit of $64 billion. But it soon became apparent that the FY 1990 performance was heading deeper into the red than anticipated. The eventual deficit was $221 billion, not $93 billion as forecast. Revised projections also indicated an even bigger imbalance in FY 1991. The erratic estimates were largely due to two factors. The bailout of the savings and loan industry, enacted in 1989, was proving to be a huge burden. Total costs were heading toward $500 billion, far above the original estimate of $148 billion. Meanwhile, the economy was showing signs of slowing down, so tax receipts were falling well short of optimistic estimates. It was no longer possible to manipulate fiscal projections to sustain the illusion that G-R-H targets were being met. There was also growing concern that the extra-large deficit, coming at a time when interest rates were rising worldwide, would force up U.S. interest rates to unacceptable levels. The new crisis compelled the White House and Democratic congressional leaders to adopt a more responsible attitude. Even so, working out a new budgetary agreement proved to be an arduous process.

Bush now recognized that taxes would have to be raised, but he sought to cover himself against charges of betraying his 1988 election pledge by getting the Democrats to take the initiative in proposing this. Not surprisingly, the opposition party had no interest in saving him from embarrassment. Democratic leaders wanted the president publicly to acknowledge that new taxes were necessary as a precondition to beginning budget talks. Once this hurdle was negotiated, it took another three months to work out a detailed agreement. Eventually Bush relinquished his demand for a cut in the capital gains tax (which he wanted in order to boost the flagging economy), and the Democrats agreed that income taxes for the wealthy would not be increased. The final package featured higher excise taxes, particularly on gasoline and home heating oil, and domestic spending cuts, which fell heavily on the Medicare program.

This compromise soon displeased the rank and file of

both parties in Congress. Conservative Republicans were furious that Bush had reneged on his election promise, while many Democrats objected that the Medicare economies and higher excise taxes would hurt the less advantaged. As a result, the House of Representatives rejected the enabling legislation in early October, with the majority in both parties voting against it. The outcome was a severe blow to Bush's leadership image. Fearful of further alienating his own party, he held back from direct involvement in negotiating a new package. This allowed Democratic leaders leeway to come up with proposals acceptable to their side. The result was a more liberal measure that increased tax rates on the wealthy and reduced their tax-deduction allowances but scaled down the Medicare economies and the gasoline tax hike. This carried both houses with heavy Democratic support. It was anticipated that the revised plan would reduce the projected deficit by $490 billion over five years.

The 1990 budget package was the toughest deficit-reduction measure yet enacted. The Republican right never forgave Bush: it bitterly resented his failure to fight harder for bigger cuts in spending and regarded his acceptance of the tax increase as a symbolic rejection of the Reagan legacy. Yet he deserved credit for doing what Ronald Reagan had never done—recognizing that strong antideficit action was necessary and incurring the political risks involved. A further sign of the new desire for fiscal discipline was the enactment of the Budget Enforcement Act of 1990 to replace the G-R-H process. Unlike its predecessor, this did not set targets for deficit reduction but sought zero-program budgeting through FY 1995. The overriding aim was to impose spending restraint in a more orderly and practical manner than G-R-H had achieved. Henceforth budget increases in entitlements, other domestic programs, and defense had to be offset by compensatory cuts from other programs in the same category or by tax increases. The sole exception to this rule involved emergency spending, defined as "expenditure that is urgent, sudden, and unforeseen, and is not permanent." Only the president could determine when such spending was necessary.

The pity was that the good effects of the 1990 budget measures were soon overtaken by the 1991–1992 recession. The automatic fiscal results of economic decline—depressed tax receipts and rising outlays on unemployment insurance and other entitlements—produced record deficits in FY 1991 and FY 1992. The recession was not the only economic problem affecting the budget. Many American firms, like General Motors and IBM, faced intense pressures in an increasingly competitive global economy and were slimming down their work forces to save on production costs. Some analysts gloomily predicted that the United States had become locked into a vicious circle whereby a sluggish economy, rising public debt, and high real interest rates would reinforce each other and keep the deficit rising for years to come. In their view there was a serious danger that the budget would be more than $600 billion in the red by the end of the century.

In spite of the renewed seriousness of the budgetary situation, neither of the main political parties made deficit reduction a key issue in the 1992 election. The state of the economy dominated the presidential campaign. George Bush promised no further tax increases and cuts in some taxes, such as capital gains, to stimulate recovery from the recession. Governor Bill Clinton of Arkansas was determined to establish his credentials as a "new" Democrat rather than a "tax and spend" one. Clinton's *Putting People First* plan for economic renewal downplayed budgetary problems in its claim that economic growth would cut the deficit in half by the end of his first term as president. To boost the economy, he proposed to increase spending on public infrastructure projects, education, and training, and to introduce a national health insurance system. How this would be paid for remained a mystery. Clinton proposed to raise taxes only on the wealthy but promised to reduce the tax burden of middle-income families.

The only candidate seriously to address the deficit problem in the 1992 presidential election was a self-professed non-politician. The central plank of Texan billionaire Ross Perot's independent campaign was his plan to balance the budget by 1998. This required the elimination of discretionary spending on "nonessential" programs (such as the space station and the Rural Electrification Administration), the termination of many tax write-offs and the imposition of a ceiling on mortgage interest deductions, the reduction of farm subsidies, a slimmed-down post–cold war military establishment, increases in gasoline and tobacco taxes, more efficient collection of taxes, and a means-tested approach to Social Security and Medicare entitlements. Perot's impact on the election was substantial. A grass-roots movement was organized to support him, and his personal fortune paid for half-hour "info-mercials" on network television to explain his ideas. In winning 19 percent of the national vote, Perot performed better than any third-party or independent presidential candidate since 1912. His showing probably owed more to the antipolitician mood of a recession-battered electorate than to popular approval of the specifics of his program. Nevertheless, he had done more than anyone to alert his fellow citizens to the dimensions of the budgetary crisis.

Once the euphoria of the campaign was over, Clinton

himself came to believe that deficit reduction should have top priority. Even though the economy had come out of recession in the last quarter of 1992, the new president was persuaded by his economic advisers that the rise in government borrowing would keep real interest rates at a high level, thus harming private investment and productivity. Probably the most influential voice was that of Federal Reserve chairman Alan Greenspan, who warned of eventual financial catastrophe. According to his projections, the deficit problem would appear to recede over the next two or three years because defense spending was scheduled to fall now that the cold war was over. But the outlook changed drastically after 1996. At that point, Greenspan predicted, rising entitlement and social program costs would inflate the deficit, and interest on the debt would explode. The effect of this on general interest rates would render the whole financial system unstable. In effect Clinton was being told that he might become another Herbert Hoover with his presidency destroyed by a catastrophe akin to that of 1931. This could hardly fail to resonate with him. The only way to avoid such a fate, Greenspan urged, was to act now. Clinton therefore set aside his agenda of economic renewal to spend much of his first year in office in the political struggle to enact yet another deficit-reduction plan.

Building on the foundations laid by Perot, Clinton used the presidential bully pulpit to mold popular support for his program. In the spring of 1993 one poll recorded 55 percent support for the view that taxes would have to be raised to reduce the deficit. This represented a marked difference from the Reagan era. Nevertheless, Clinton still encountered great difficulty in persuading Congress to support him. His budget plan passed the House of Representatives by only two votes and the Senate by one vote in August. Republicans and conservative Democrats objected that the mix of tax increases and spending cuts tilted too much toward taxes, while liberal Democrats charged that it was weighted too heavily toward cutbacks. The strength of opposition had already been signaled by the earlier defeat of a jobs-stimulation program that formed part of Clinton's original budget plan. In these circumstances the administration was forced to make significant concessions. Clinton agreed to a total cap on discretionary social spending and to divert any new tax revenues into deficit reduction rather than spending programs. In addition, he substituted an increase in gasoline taxes in place of his proposal for a broad energy tax intended to promote conservation and reduce the country's dependence on foreign oil.

The final measure sought total deficit reduction of $494 billion over five years by raising $241 billion in new taxes and saving $255 billion through spending cuts. Clinton's tax program entailed a significant reversal of Reaganomics. The top rate of income tax was raised to 36 percent (and a further surcharge of 10 percent imposed on taxable personal income over $250,000), Medicare payroll taxes were increased for the wealthy by removing the $135,000 ceiling on taxable income, Social Security benefits for middle- and upper-income groups were made subject to higher taxation, and gasoline taxes were again raised. It was estimated that Americans with an annual income in excess of $200,000 would bear over 80 percent of these tax increases. The position of middle-income groups would be largely unaffected other than by the higher gasoline tax, while tax credits for the low-paid would result in lower tax burdens for many households with an income of under $27,000 a year. On the spending side, Medicare and Medicaid, the farm program, and foreign aid took large cuts. Taking advantage of the post–cold war peace dividend, the military was scheduled to take bigger cuts than the Bush administration had projected. Clinton also shelved plans to increase spending on programs that had suffered neglect in the 1980s. The most significant casualty was the kind of public investment expenditure that he had emphasized in his election campaign.

Clinton had succeeded in enacting the most complicated and ambitious deficit-reduction measure in American history in the face of unanimous opposition from Republican congressmen and with only lukewarm support from his fellow Democrats. The price of failure would have been high, both in economic and political terms. Having invested his prestige in the battle to enact the plan, he would have been hard-pressed to rescue his presidency from the consequences of defeat.

Yet the political fruits of victory were scarcely bountiful. Clinton had staked everything on averting a future catastrophe, so he did not reap the kind of reward that resulted from successful management of an immediate crisis. The long battle with Congress had hurt his standing with the public, for it signified that the restoration of one-party control of national government had not ended political gridlock. Also, Clinton had spent most of first year in office on an issue that could never provide his administration with a positive theme, rather than in building up support for his economic renewal program. To make matters worse, deficit reduction took resources away from his planned revolution in public investment. Thus it was hardly surprising that many Americans were uncertain what Clinton's presidency stood for. This was to hurt him when he belatedly began to fight for health care and other parts of his agenda during his second year in office. Nevertheless, whatever his achievements as president, Clinton's historical significance may well have been guaranteed by his successful battle for deficit reduction.

The new plan showed immediate signs of being more successful than the 1990 model. It benefited from a more favorable economic climate than its predecessor. Recovery from the recession saw the FY 1993 deficit fall to $254 billion. The deficit reduction program helped to sustain this trend in FY 1994. For FY 1995 Clinton found himself in the happy position of being able to submit a deficit estimate in the executive budget of just $176 billion, more than $100 billion below what he had projected a year earlier. There now seemed a good chance that he would come close to fulfilling his election promise to cut the deficit in half by the end of his first term. Equally important, the size of the deficit in relationship to the economy was in decline from its peak level of 4.9 percent in FY 1992 to an estimated level of 2.4 percent in FY 1995.

## BEYOND THE RED PERIL

The federal budget can never be considered in isolation from the American economy. The success of Clinton's deficit-reduction plan would eventually be measured in terms of its contribution to national economic renewal. In other words, the program was a means to an end rather than an end in itself. Signs were that the red peril of monster deficits had been brought under control. Nevertheless, a strong belief persisted in some circles that more needed to be done to eliminate the deficit altogether. The Concord Coalition—organized by former Democratic senator Paul Tsongas, former Republican senator Warren Rudman, and investment banker and former government official Peter G. Peterson—called for an austerity approach of spending cuts and tax increases to balance the budget. Ross Perot and many conservatives in both political parties sought the same goal, but only by reducing expenditures. Yet it would serve little purpose for the U.S. government to become caught up in a new fascination for budget balancing. According to a report issued in 1994 by the Congressional Budget Office, it would require $743 billion in expenditure reduction (or a combination of spending cuts and tax increases) to get the budget into the black by the end of this century. The evidence suggests that this would damage rather than help the economy.

Few would question that deficit reduction was necessary in the early 1990s to safeguard the future well-being of the American economy. There was a real danger that the day of reckoning would come, regardless of whether it happened in the last decade of the twentieth century or early in the next century, unless corrective action was undertaken. This was underlined by projections in the 1992 report, *Reducing the Deficit: Spending and Revenue Options*, by the nonpartisan General Accounting Office (GAO) of Congress. Using computer simulations, the GAO estimated that if the deficit were allowed to rise as a share of GNP at the same rate as in the Reagan-Bush years, it would reach 20.6 percent by 2020. Annual interest on the national debt would then consume 31.5 percent of the budget, the proportion now taken by Social Security and health care. The United States would be reduced to Third World debtor status in terms of its debt-GNP ratio. Even if the deficit were held steady at 3 percent of GNP, the growing cost of interest on the national debt would eventually cause huge problems. "After 2005," the GAO predicted, "the amount of deficit reduction action required annually to stay on the 3% path increases exponentially. Measured in constant dollars, it exceeds half a trillion dollars by 2020 and is still rising."

Whether the United States needs to balance the budget—as

opposed to bringing the deficit under control—is a more controversial issue. Advocates of a balanced budget contend it is the only way to boost economic growth, which they believe is being held back by inadequate private investment. To them, the root of the problem is insufficient savings, because government borrowing must be financed from private savings that would otherwise be used for productive invest-ment in business, technology, and research and development. Admittedly, a dollar cut from the deficit does not auto-matically translate into another dollar in national savings. According to some estimates, the yield would be around seventy cents, because many people would use some of their savings to pay for higher tax bills or to make up for cuts in government services. Moreover, in an open, global economy, up to half the increase in national savings could actually go into investment abroad. Nevertheless, a significant portion would be available for domestic investment.

Yet the theory that a balanced budget will make the nation significantly richer is a dubious one. A detailed study by the Federal Reserve Bank of New York estimated that economic output would have been only 3 percent higher in real terms if every budget of the Reagan-Bush era had been balanced. This calculation was based on the following reasoning. The national debt rose from $994 billion to $4 trillion between FY 1981 and FY 1992. If the federal government had not operated a single deficit during this period, its borrowing needs would have been $3 trillion less than they actually were. What if this entire sum—equivalent to half of one year's output by the U.S. economy—had gone into private investment? The average real rate of return on private assets during the Reagan-Bush years was 6 percent. Since the total accumulation of debt equaled half of one year's output, the return on an equivalent amount of investment would have been 6 percent times one-half—in other words, 3 percent of GNP.

For different reasons, Keynesians too are critical of budget-balancing as a strategy for economic renewal. In their view, the notion that private saving is the main determinant of private investment harks back to classical economics. The 1930s taught Keynesians a different lesson: that it is the prospect of future profits, not the supply of current savings, which is fundamentally necessary for high investment. From their perspective, the real cause of the low investment of recent times has been the sluggish performance of the American economy since 1973. In a recent book, University of Nebraska economist Wallace Peterson went so far as to claim that the economy has been in the grip of a "silent depression" for the last twenty years. The characteristics of this phenomenon were a decline of nearly one-fifth in the real weekly income of the American worker between 1973 and 1990, a relatively high level of unemployment, and slow productivity growth.

If this diagnosis is accurate, an austerity drive to balance the budget would weaken an economy already suffering from long-term stagnation. In fact, a study by the St. Louis Federal Reserve Bank indicated that the principal cause for the post-1989 increase in the deficit was the sharp slowdown in the rate of growth of federal tax receipts in a sluggish economy. It follows, therefore, that economic growth would provide a stronger foundation—in the form of enhanced revenues—for holding down the deficit than would austerity measures. In the view of many Keynesians, the budget should be an essential instrument for bringing this about.

In contrast to the new economists of the 1960s, the Keynesian advocates of progrowth policies in the 1990s do not regard full employment as an economic elixir. In the postwar era most jobs were full time and provided adequate income. This is no longer the case. Just over half the new jobs created between 1979 and 1987 paid an annual wage below the poverty level. Accordingly, supporters of expansionary fiscal policy now insist that a full-employment strategy must seek the creation not simply of jobs but of decent-paying jobs. As an interim measure they believe that the Earned Income Tax Credit contained in the 1994 deficit-reduction program should be expanded to provide low-income workers with extra cash. In the long term they recognize that improved productivity is vital to provide adequately paid jobs and that only increased investment can achieve this. Thus the new Keynesianism of the 1990s regards an expansion of public investment in economic infrastructure and human capital as an essential spur to private investment.

In 1992 New York investment banker Felix Rohatyn suggested that the federal government needed to spend $1 trillion over the next ten to fifteen years to supplement state and local government spending on economic infrastructure projects. This policy proposal would restore public infra-structure spending to about 3.5 percent of national output, the average level between 1950 and 1975. It was about twice the annual expenditure rate envisioned over a four-year period by Bill Clinton's *Putting People First* campaign document, a projection that was significantly scaled down in the 1994 deficit-reduction plan. Other analysts place equal emphasis on the need for better education and training to improve the quality and skills of the American work force and for health-care reform to provide decent medical treatment at an affordable price, so reducing the huge proportion of national economic resources (18.2 percent of per capita disposable income in 1992) consumed by health spending.

Can such ambitious measures be realized without once more unleashing the red peril of higher deficits and debt? The extra revenues generated by economic growth would offset some of the costs. Further tax increases could pay for bigger spending, but the political unpopularity of this policy effectively rules out its enactment. Higher taxes would also have the negative effect of slowing economic growth. The alternative approach is to change the composition of federal spending.

Many Keynesians believe that huge savings can be made on national defense. Notwithstanding planned reductions, they contend that the United States still maintains a level of military power more than sufficient to meet any imaginable need in the post–cold war era. A peace dividend of further defense economies worth $100 billion would provide resources for the revitalization of infrastructure investment. Critics respond that military retrenchment has already gone too far and weakened America's influence in global politics. In their view, the most suitable target for spending cutbacks is the social welfare budget, especially through the introduction of means-testing for Social Security and Medicare entitlements to prevent the affluent from receiving benefits that they do not really need. The debate over budgetary policy is further muddied by the preference of most Republicans and conservative Democrats to boost growth by cutting taxes and financing this within a balanced budget by means of spending reductions.

Republican success in winning control of both houses of Congress for the first time in forty years in 1994 dimmed the prospects of the public investment revolution. But whether this victory heralded the emergence of a new fiscal consensus is unclear. The GOP manifesto, Contract with America, promised tax reduction (notably a $500 credit for every child in a taxpaying family and the halving of the capital gains tax on business) and a balanced budget. Reconciling these pledges would be difficult, particularly as the Republicans also wished to increase defense spending and revive the Strategic Defense Initiative project. Cutting welfare, the prime target of many conservatives, would only meet part of the costs of this fiscal agenda. Congress would face tough choices as to where else in the domestic budget to wield the axe. Perhaps it would not flinch from making these choices, but failure to do so might result in another dangerous enlargement of the federal deficit, as happened in the 1980s.

## THE HISTORICAL RECORD

The historian can only analyze what has happened rather than what might happen. As the United States contemplates its budgetary future, it is useful to examine the fiscal record of the last sixty years. A historical assessment of deficit government must recognize that the budget is more than just a tally sheet of outlays and receipts. It is and always has been a vital expression of the responsibilities of government. Its fundamental purposes are to pay for programs that the nation needs, to manage the economy, and to raise revenue in an equitable manner. Although the United States has few balanced budgets to its credit during the last two-thirds of a century, it has been more successful in achieving a balance between the various purposes of budgetary policy.

With the exception of the Truman-Eisenhower era, the U.S. government has not paid its way since the 1920s. On the more lax standard of deficit control, however, it has a much better record. Roosevelt's deficits in the 1930s were modest ones. Those in the 1940s were huge only because of the exceptional circumstances of World War II. When deficits were incurred during the postwar quarter-century, they were almost invariably small. The only two large deficits in this period, in FY 1959 and FY 1968, were isolated instances and were both followed by a balanced budget. Though deficits grew in dollar terms in the 1970s, they were relatively modest as a proportion of GNP, excepting the recession years in mid-decade. Only in the 1980s and early 1990s was there real loss of control over the budget deficit. The measures undertaken during the Bush and Clinton presidencies offer hope that this was a temporary breakdown.

The budget had also been an important instrument of economic management since the 1930s. Roosevelt was a hesitant Keynesian who took too long to commit himself to a strong course of action. His fiscal policy during the Depression was arguably more successful in political than economic terms. Though Truman's Keynesian credentials were never seriously tested by recession, he proved adept in using the budget to stifle inflation. Eisenhower scored high marks for his antiinflation record, but his obsession with price stability caused him to underestimate the dangers of recession in the latter part of his presidency. The new economics of the Kennedy-Johnson era closed the performance gap that had developed in the economy and brought about full employment. While it was appreciably less successful in the task of economic restraint, the inflation rate in the late 1960s looks far less serious when viewed from the present day than it did at the time.

In spite of stagflation, fiscal policy could claim some success in the 1970s. Deficits did far more economic good than harm during this decade. The Republican administrations of Nixon and Ford used the full-employment budget, admittedly with limited enthusiasm, to counter the effects of recession. Jimmy Carter's reluctance to make more positive use of this instrument of economic activism helped to lose him the White House in 1980. Fiscal policy failed to curb inflation in the 1970s, but only Nixon was guilty of stoking up demand pressures. The main sources of price instability were supply-shocks and cost-push pressures that were unrelated to the budget. Ronald Reagan proved the greatest Keynesian of all in the 1981–1982 recession, though inadvertently so. But his record as an economic manager was the worst among modern presidents because his huge post-recession deficits had a deleterious effect on national saving, interest rates, and the trade deficit. This legacy contributed to the economic problems that undermined the Bush presidency.

Budgetary expansion also went hand-in-hand with the growing responsibilities of American government. The New Deal never spent enough, nor did it always spend wisely. Nevertheless, it laid the foundations of the modern welfare state and the investor state. In the postwar era the Truman and Eisenhower administrations sustained the development of domestic programs inherited from the New Deal but gave overwhelming priority to waging the cold war. Thanks to the harvest of revenue generated by the progrowth strategy of the new economics, the United States was able simultaneously to finance a substantial expansion of domestic and defense programs in the 1960s for the only time in its history.

In the economically troubled 1970s the growth of the welfare state and the investor state was sustained through the transference of resources from national security. The pendulum swung sharply in the opposite direction in the 1980s. Real military outlays were restored to what they had been at the height of the Korean and Vietnam wars. To compensate for this, the Reagan administration sought domestic cutbacks, but the axe fell on well-established programs. In particular, the relative decline of expenditure on physical resource programs undermined the development of public capital projects that were vital to sustain long-term economic growth. Retrenchment also hit the social programs serving the neediest groups in society. Moreover, the huge deficits run up by Reagan made it virtually impossible to develop new spending programs to address the changing needs of society.

Tax policy was also successful for the most part from the 1940s to the late 1970s. Roosevelt's wartime establishment of a modern, progressive system of taxation made up for the New Deal's regressive record. It also provided the revenue base to sustain the growth of federal spending in the postwar era within the framework of a balanced budget. For a brief time in the mid-1960s the United States was nearly in the position of being able to afford both the expansion of government and the reduction of taxes. But in the 1970s the bracket-creep consequences of inflation generated a rising tax burden. The resulting pressure for income tax reduction caused a shift in tax policy away from progressivity that reached full flow in the 1980s. The tax structure put in place by Reagan remains largely intact. Some analysts believe that its reform is essential to enhance the prospects of economic renewal. The current system places a disproportionate burden on lower-income and middle-income groups. Notwithstanding the 1994 tax increases, the tax obligations of those with high incomes are still well below what they were in 1977. Liberal critics of the current tax system claim that the restoration of progressivity would help to correct the maldistribution of income, one of the primary aspects of post-1973 economic stagnation, and provide a larger volume of revenue to pay for government. The contrary opinion is that this would only serve to discourage saving and investment.

The 1980s saw another significant change in tax policy. A strong link had been maintained between taxing and spending from 1945 until the late 1970s. The tax cut of 1948 was enacted at a time when the budget operated a large surplus. In the 1950s Eisenhower resisted his own party's desire for tax reduction and sustained several of the supposedly temporary Korean War taxes in order to achieve balanced budgets. Fear of incurring a big deficit made Kennedy a hesitant convert to the new economics. His successor chose to reduce spending in order to facilitate eventual enactment of the 1964 tax cut. Four years later, with a presidential election looming, Johnson had no hesitation in demanding a temporary tax increase to eliminate the Vietnam-related deficit. Inflation began to erode the political nexus between the tax and spending sides of the budget in the second half of the 1970s, even though Carter did his best to resist this. It was the tax cuts of 1981 that finally broke the link and ushered in the era of big deficits.

In sum, budgetary policy was generally successful for much of the age of deficits. Before the 1980s unbalanced budgets helped to finance the growing responsibilities of the federal government in modern society. They did not result from a tax policy that blatantly favored upper-income groups. They were beneficial to the economy. More often than not, deficits were problematic when they were too small rather than too big, as was the case in the 1930s, the late 1950s, and the late 1970s. Arguably, the reverse was true only in 1967–1968 and 1972. In spite of the relative failure on inflation, budgetary policy was most successful in the Kennedy-Johnson era of the 1960s. Unquestionably the opposite was the case in the Reagan era of the 1980s. Whether deficit government can ever be made to work as well again as in the past remains to be seen. But recent failures should not be allowed to overshadow its half-century of success.

# Recommended Reading

The first significant effort to examine the budget in historical perspective was Lewis H. Kimmel, *Federal Budget and Fiscal Policy, 1789–1958* (Washington, D.C., 1959). This classic study has been superseded by several recent works. Herbert Stein charts the post-1933 development of fiscal policy in *The Fiscal Revolution in America* (Chicago, 1969) and *Presidential Economics: The Making of Economic Policy from Roosevelt to Reagan and Beyond* (New York, 1985); James D. Savage examines the political symbolism of deficits from colonial times to the present in *Balanced Budgets and American Politics* (Ithaca, N.Y., 1988); and Dennis S. Ippolito examines budget control in *Uncertain Legacies: Federal Budget Policy from Roosevelt Through Reagan* (Charlottesville, Va., 1990).

No one has yet produced a monographic survey of Franklin D. Roosevelt's budget policy. Several general works nevertheless offer useful insights into this subject, notably James MacGregor Burns, *Roosevelt: The Lion and the Fox* (New York, 1956); Richard Polenberg, *War and Society: The United States, 1941–1945* (Philadelphia, 1972); Peter Fearon, *War, Prosperity and Depression: The U.S. Economy, 1917–45* (Lawrence, Kans., 1987); and Anthony J. Badger, *The New Deal: The Depression Years, 1933–1940* (New York, 1989). The development of fiscal policy is analyzed by Dean L. May, *From New Deal to New Economics: The American Liberal Response to the Recession of 1937* (New York, 1981); Alan Brinkley "The New Deal and the Idea of the State," in Steve Fraser and Gary Gerstle, eds., *The Rise and Fall of the New Deal Order, 1930–1980* (Princeton, 1989), pp. 85–121; and Richard P. Adelstein, "'The Nation as an Economic Unit': Keynes, Roosevelt, and the Managerial Ideal," *Journal of*

*American History*, 78 (June 1991), 160–187. On tax reform, Mark H. Leff, *The Limits of Symbolic Reform: The New Deal and Taxation, 1933–1939* (New York, 1984) is indispensable and can be supplemented by John Witte's less accessible study, *The Politics and Development of the Federal Income Tax* (Madison, Wisc., 1985).

Truman's budget policy also lacks a monographic study but is usefully covered by Alonzo L. Hamby, *Beyond the New Deal: Harry S. Truman and American Liberalism* (New York, 1973); Robert Donovan, *Conflict and Crisis: The Presidency of Harry S. Truman, 1945–1948* and *Tumultuous Years: The Presidency of Harry S. Truman, 1949–1953* (New York, 1977 and 1982); and Donald McCoy, *The Presidency of Harry S. Truman* (Lawrence, Kans., 1984). Eisenhower-era fiscal history is discussed in two studies by Iwan W. Morgan, *Eisenhower versus "The Spenders": The Eisenhower Administration, the Democrats and the Budget, 1953–60* (New York, 1990), and "Eisenhower and the Balanced Budget," in Shirley Anne Warshaw, ed., *Reexamining the Eisenhower Presidency* (Westport, Conn., 1993), pp. 121–132, and by John W. Sloan, *Eisenhower and the Management of Prosperity* (Lawrence, Kans., 1991). For defense-related issues, Stephen Ambrose, *Eisenhower: The President, 1952–1969* (New York, 1984) is excellent.

Allen J. Matusow, *The Unraveling of America: A History of Liberalism in the 1960s* (New York, 1984) offers an excellent analysis of the new economics within the context of 1960s liberalism. Irving Bernstein, *Promises Kept: John F. Kennedy's New Frontier* (New York, 1991) has a good chapter on the 1964 tax cut, and Lyndon B. Johnson, *The Vantage Point: Perspectives on the Presidency, 1963–1969* (New York, 1971) is useful—though self-serving—on the 1968 tax increase. Walter H. Heller, *New Dimensions of Political Economy* (New York, 1966) is a confident exposition of the new economics at its peak. For more sober but still laudatory assessments, see Arthur M. Okun, *The Political Economy of Prosperity* (Washington, D.C., 1970), and James

Tobin, *The New Economics One Decade Older* (Princeton, 1974).
For Vietnam, see Anthony Campagna, *The Economic Consequences of the Vietnam War* (New York, 1991).

For political economy in the 1970s, consult Alan S. Blinder, *Economic Policy and the Great Stagflation* (New York, 1979); Douglas Hibbs, *The American Political Economy: Macroeconomics and Electoral Politics* (Cambridge, Mass., 1987); and Iwan W. Morgan, *Beyond the Liberal Consensus: A Political History of the United States Since 1965* (New York, 1994). The policies of specific administrations are discussed in A. James Reichley, *Conservatives in an Age of Change: The Nixon-Ford Administrations* (Washington, D.C., 1981); John W. Sloan, "Groping Towards a Macrotheme: Economic Policymaking in the Ford Presidency," in Bernard J. Firestone and Alexej Urinsky, eds., *Gerald R. Ford and the Politics of Post-Watergate America*, I (Westport, Conn., 1993), 245–275; and Burton I. Kaufman, *The Presidency of James Earl Carter Jr.* (Lawrence, Kans., 1993). For executive-legislative conflicts over the budget, see James L. Sundquist, *The Decline and Resurgence of Congress* (Washington, D.C., 1981).

For useful, brief introductions to the 1980s, see Joseph Hogan, "The Federal Budget in the Reagan Era" in Joseph Hogan, ed., *The Reagan Years: The Record in Presidential Leadership* (Manchester, England, 1989), pp. 214–236, and Paul E. Peterson and Mark Rom, "Lower Taxes, More Spending and Budget Deficits," in Charles O. Jones, ed., *The Reagan Legacy: Promise and Performance* (Chatham, N.J., 1988), pp. 213–240. For a highly critical perspective on the Reagan deficits, see Benjamin Friedman, *Day of Reckoning: The Consequences of American Economic Policy Under Reagan and After* (New York, 1988). Robert Eisner, *How Real Is the Federal Deficit?* (New York, 1986), represents the "benign deficit" school. Ronald Reagan, *An American Life: The Autobiography* (New York, 1990) contains revealing snippets on budgetary policy. Other memoirs that throw important light on the same subject include David

Stockman, *The Triumph of Politics* (New York, 1986), and Paul Craig Roberts, *The Supply-Side Revolution: An Insider's Account of Policymaking in Washington* (Cambridge, Mass., 1984). For insightful discussions of Congress in the Reagan years, see Aaron Wildavsky, *The New Politics of the Budgetary Process* (Glenview, Ill., 1988), and Rudolph G. Penner and Alan J. Abramson, *Broken Purse Strings: Congressional Budgeting, 1974–1988* (Washington, D.C., 1989).

Colin Campbell, S.J., and Bert A. Rockman, eds., *The Bush Presidency: First Appraisals* (Chatham, N.J., 1991) is good on presidential-congressional relations on the budget in the early 1990s. Bob Woodward, *The Agenda: Inside the Clinton White House* (New York, 1994) is an intriguing fly-on-the-wall account of the design and enactment of the 1994 deficit-reduction package. For illuminating but differing accounts of the American economy, see Wallace C. Peterson, *Silent Depression: The Fate of the American Dream* (New York, 1994), and Paul Krugman, *Peddling Prosperity: Economic Sense and Nonsense in the Age of Diminished Expectations* (New York, 1994).

# Index

Ackley, Gardner, 109, 110
Ambrose, Stephen, 70
Anderson, Robert, 83

Balanced budget amendment, 161–162
*Bowsher v Synar*, 167
Budget reforms: 1921, 13–14; 1974, 21, 136, 141, 159; 1990, 186–187. *See also* Gramm-Rudman-Hollings.
Bureau of the Budget (BOB), 14, 107. *See also* Office of Management and Budget.
Burns, James MacGregor, 40
Bush, George, ix, 12, 183, 187; and deficit reduction, 184–186, 199
Business, 90, 91–92; and deficits, 27, 52–53, 77–78; and taxes, 44, 46, 93, 146

Califano, Joseph A., 130
Carter, Jimmy, ix, 137, 142, 147, 150, 156, 158, 171; fiscal policy of, 127–134, 199; and taxes, 134, 145–146, 202
Catchings, Waddill, 37
Chase, Stuart, 37

Civil War, 4, 8
Civil Works Administration (CWA), 32–33
Clinton, Bill, 182, 184, 187–188; and deficit reduction, 189–192, 199
Committee for Economic Development, 52–53, 77
Congress: and budget-making, 13, 14–15, 31, 136, 137–138, 159–160, 161, 163–165, 166–168, 184–186, 189–191; conservative coalition in, 40–41, 48–49, 50, 72, 84, 88–89, 101, 106; and defense spending, 64, 70, 99–100, 141; and taxes, 23, 50–51, 93–94, 111–113, 145–146, 197
Congressional Budget Office, 136, 193
Corporate taxes, 6–7, 46–47, 49–51, 61, 62, 144, 145–146, 151, 164, 165, 166, 168
Council of Economic Advisers (CEA), 78, 88–91, 92, 95, 101, 108–111, 113–114, 119
Currie, Lauchlin, 37

Darman, Richard, 14

Defense spending, 11, 47–48, 63–71, 95–100, 138, 140–142, 159, 169–172, 197–198

Deficits, 10, 18, 198; pre-1930s, 3–6; in Great Depression, 19, 21–31, 37–41; in World War II, 47, 52–53; in postwar era, 56, 58–59, 62–63, 66, 77, 79–80, 82–84, 199; in 1960s, 89, 90–93, 94, 106, 110, 113, 202; in 1970s, 119–120, 122, 125, 127, 130, 131–133, 134, 135, 137, 140, 142; in Reagan era, 148, 149–150, 152, 155, 157, 160, 161–169, 174–181, 202; in 1990s and beyond, 182, 184–185, 186, 187–188, 189, 192, 193, 195

Democrats, 20–21, 40–41, 62, 63, 75, 139, 160; and defense spending, 64, 69, 70, 71, 141–142, 170; and deficit reduction, 164, 175–176, 184–186, 189–190, 197; fiscal policy of, 82, 83–84, 125–127; and taxes, 23, 127, 134, 145, 155, 164

Dewey, Thomas E., 52

Dillon, Douglas, 93

Douglas, Lewis, 29, 32

Dukakis, Michael, 183

Eccles, Marriner, 36, 37

Economic Recovery Tax Act (ERTA, 1946), 150–151, 154, 155–157, 164, 165

Eisenhower, Dwight D., ix, 55, 87, 89, 91, 96, 126, 129, 198; and balanced budgets, 12, 56, 58–59, 84; and defense spending, 67–71, 97; and domestic program spending, 72, 73–76, 200; fiscal policy of, 79–85, 150, 199; and taxes, 61–63, 201

Eisner, Robert, 177

Employment Act (1946), 77–78, 79, 80

Energy taxes, 150, 165

Excise taxes, 4, 42–43, 61, 185, 186

Ezekiel, Mordecai, 37

Farley, James, 36

Farm programs, 30, 34–35, 43, 74, 172, 190

Feldstein, Martin, 174

Federal Emergency Relief Administration, 32–33

Federal Finance Bank, 137–138

Federal Reserve, 16–17, 51, 52, 81, 112, 113–114; and Great Depression, 20, 22–23, 26, 35; and stagflation, 119, 121, 130, 133, 154–155, 158. *See also* Monetary policy.

Ford, Gerald, ix, 133, 134, 140, 141, 146; fiscal policy of, 123–127, 199

Foster, William Truffant, 37

Friedman, Milton, 174

Full-employment budget, 11, 25, 89, 121, 177, 199

General Accounting Office, 167, 193
Great Depression, 11, 20–21, 178
Gold: reserves, 22, 26, 35–36, 52, 112; exchange standard, 87–88, 116, 120
Great Society, 101–107, 108, 172
Greenspan, Alan, 126, 189
Gramm, Phil, 166, 167
Gramm-Rudman-Hollings, 166–168, 171, 184, 186

Hansen, Alvin, 53
Heller, Walter, 88–90
Henderson, Leon, 37
Hobson, J. A., 37
Hollings, Ernest, 166, 175
Hoover, Herbert, 131, 149, 189; and deficit budgets, 21–22, 24, 25, 27, 29, 41
Hopkins, Harry, 29, 32, 33–34, 36
Humphrey, George, 62–63, 69
Humphrey-Hawkins full employment bill, 127, 130
Humphrey, Hubert, 10

Ickes, Harold, 29, 36–37
Inflation, 11–12, 77, 109, 116, 122, 199; and deficits, 27, 59, 80–81, 111, 114, 124–125, 126–127, 130, 131–133

Ippolito, Dennis, 64
Interstate highway program, 74–75, 105

Jefferson, Thomas, 8
Johnson, Hugh, 29
Johnson, Lyndon B., ix, 13–14, 60, 86, 150, 199, 202; and defense spending, 97–100; and Great Society, 101, 102, 103, 106–107, 108; tax policy of, 94, 110–114, 151, 201–202

Kemp, Jack, 146, 153, 164
Kennedy, Edward, 130, 134
Kennedy, John, ix, 71, 85, 86; and defense spending, 95–97; fiscal policy of, 88–94, 150, 151, 199, 201, 202
Kennedy, Robert, 107
Keynesianism, 8, 11, 30, 127–128, 151, 152, 177, 195–196, 197; in the 1930s, 37–40; and World War II, 52–54, 77–78. See also New economics.
Keynes, John Maynard, 37–38, 89, 95, 151
Kissinger, Henry, 70
Korean War, 60–61, 62, 66, 100, 135, 159, 170, 200, 201

Laffer, Arthur, 146, 152
La Follette, Robert, 33, 46
Leff, Mark, 46
Lincoln, Abraham, 8

Line-item veto, 161–162
Long, Huey, 44

McGovern, George, 121
McNamara, Robert, 96–97, 99
Matusow, Allen, 110
Medicare. *See* Social insurance programs.
Mellon, Andrew, 9
Mills, Wilbur, 112
Moley, Raymond, 29
Mondale, Walter, 130, 165, 175–176
Monetarism, 118–119
Monetary policy, 16–17, 22–23, 35, 51, 81, 87, 112, 113–114, 154. *See also* Federal Reserve.
Morgenthau, Henry, 29–30, 36, 49
Murray, James, 77
Muskie, Edmund, 127

National Advisory Commission on Civil Disorders, 107
National debt, 7–8, 51, 148, 177–180, 194
National savings, 157, 179–180
New Deal, 47, 48–49, 55, 72, 76, 83, 104, 128; and spending, 24–41; and taxes, 41–47
New economics, 11, 88–95, 101, 152, 199; and Vietnam War, 108–114
New Look, 67–69, 97
Nixon, Richard, ix, 63, 71, 83, 84, 116, 132, 134, 135–136, 140; economic policy of, 117–123, 199
NSC-68, 65–67, 70

Off-budget, 137–138, 166
Office of Management and Budget (OMB), 135, 137, 157, 158
Oil prices, 116–117, 122, 133
Okun, Arthur, 77, 94, 111
O'Neill, Thomas P. "Tip," 160, 164

Panama Canal, 5
Perkins, Frances, 29
Perot, Ross, 188, 189, 192
Personal income tax, 4, 7, 45–46, 49–51, 61, 62, 124, 144, 166, 168, 190, 201. *See also* Economic Recovery Tax Act.
Peterson, Peter, 192
Peterson, Wallace, 195
Physical resource programs, 11; spending on, 34–35, 74–76, 104–106, 139–140, 144, 172, 200
*Pollock v Farmers' Loan and Trust Co.* (1895), 7
Progressivism, 5–7, 10, 13, 28
Proposition 13, 46, 147
Public opinion: and balanced budgets, 28, 176; and taxes, 43, 50, 189

Quayle, Dan, 160

Recession, 35–36, 79–80, 82–83, 84, 119, 123–125, 131, 155, 187
Reconstruction Finance Corporation, 21, 22
Reagan, Ronald, ix, 102, 126, 131, 146, 147, 200, 202; and defense spending, 159, 169–172; and deficits, 148–150, 157–161, 162, 163, 164, 174–176, 177, 178, 179, 180, 181, 182, 183, 199–200; and taxes, 150–151, 153–154, 165–166, 200, 201
Regan, Donald, 174
Republicans, 4, 5, 9, 20–21, 40–41, 140; and defense spending, 64, 69, 70, 141–142; tax policy of, 60, 63, 127, 155, 164, 186, 189–190, 197–198
Revenue Act (1932), 22, 23, 42–43
Richberg, Donald, 29
Roberts, Paul Craig, 152
Rohatyn, Felix, 196
Roosevelt, Franklin D., ix, 12, 52, 54; and deficit spending, 23–26, 39–40, 150, 198, 199; and taxes, 41, 43, 44–46, 50–51, 200–201
Roth, William, 146
Rudman, Warren, 196

Saulnier, Raymond, 81, 83
Savage, James, 41, 134
Simon, William, 126
Social insurance programs, 30–31, 73, 102–104, 138–139, 173, 185–186, 188, 193
Social insurance taxes, 30–31, 36, 42, 44, 144, 156, 165, 173, 190
Social Security. See Social insurance programs.
Spanish-American War, 5, 8
Supply-side economics, 9, 11, 126, 146, 151–154, 177
Sputniks, 69–70
Stein, Herbert, 103
Stockman, David, 154, 158, 159, 160, 163, 174
Strategic Defense Initiative, 169, 171, 198
Strout, Richard, 84

Tariffs, 4, 5, 6, 9, 20, 42–43
Taxation, 4, 7, 9, 41–47, 59–63, 93–94, 110–114, 124–126, 142–147, 155–157, 185–187, 200–202. See also Corporate taxes; Economic Recovery Tax Act (1981); Excise taxes; Personal income taxes; Revenue Act (1931); Social insurance taxes.
Tax expenditures, 145, 156
Tobin, James, 114
Trade deficit, 116, 179–181

Treasury, 29, 35–36, 45, 51, 78, 91–92, 93, 138

Trickle-down economics, 9, 154, 157

Truman Doctrine, 64–65, 66

Truman, Harry S., ix, 55, 126, 150, 198; and balanced budgets, 56, 57–58; and defense spending, 64–67; and domestic program spending, 72–74, 200; fiscal policy of, 78–79, 199; tax policy of, 59–61

Tsongas, Paul, 192

U.S. economy, 51, 56–57, 76–77, 95, 116–117, 153, 156–157, 179–181, 187. *See also* Great Depression; Inflation; Recession; Trade deficit.

Veterans programs, 31, 49, 73

Vietnam War, 84, 86, 98–100, 102, 106–107, 109–116, 135, 140–141, 159, 170, 200

Volcker, Paul, 155

Wagner, Richard, 91

Wagner, Robert, 77

Wallace, Henry, 29, 37

Welfare programs, 31, 73–74, 102–104, 139, 172–173, 200

Williams, Aubrey, 37

Wilson, Woodrow, 6

Wirthlin, Richard, 176

Witte, John, 49

Works Progress Administration, 33–34

World War I, 7–8

World War II, 19, 47–52, 198

## A NOTE ON THE AUTHOR

Iwan W. Morgan is head of the department of politics and modern history at London Guildhall University. He studied at the University College of Wales and the London School of Economics and has written widely on American economic history. His other books include *Beyond the Liberal Consensus, America's Century,* and *Eisenhower versus "The Spenders."*